February 2018

Somewhere within the doldrums of this Louisiana winter, on a rainy-day last week, I made coffee and splurged with a cozy curl up on the couch, somewhat mindless, in front of the TV. For me, there is not much interest within the enigma of ridiculous numbers from 5 to a zillion, but I flippantly spun and finally found something, The Game Show Network.

My haphazard selection turned out to be both historical and hysterical, the perfect little undemanding stopping point in my day to have coffee and disconnect. Dick Clark was the game show host and Florence Henderson was one of the "stars". She was no longer the Brady's TV mom; she was growing out her hair and developing her game show circuit career instead. Turns out, the other team won, and, therefore, had the opportunity to make it to the top of the $25,000 Pyramid. Sadly, however, they did not. The winning contestant happily, took home just over $1000 and Florence's partner won a car, a brand new 1985 Toyota Tercel. The real car was not actually in the studio, so, they showed a picture of this beauty with California emission standards all built in. The guy that won the Tercel was so excited and, I suspect, Florence felt accomplished. I watched the entire show – best thing on TV – and walked away with an empty cup of coffee and a longing for the past.

I notice that yearning for yesterday on social media. There are FB pages that devote themselves completely to nostalgia. My husband follows one from his hometown of Miami Beach when A1A had sand on both sides of the street and he took a bus to the beach, just him and a neighborhood friend with dive knives strapped to their legs, spear guns in their hands and filled up scuba tanks on their backs; imagine getting on a city bus with that paraphernalia today! They would be gone all day without a cell phone, a credit card or an incident, just clear blue ocean water and, hopefully, fresh fish for supper. "Flipper" was being filmed in Key Biscayne and at The Miami Seaquarium then and The Magic Kingdom was s just a swamp in Florida and a vision in Walt's incredible head. The good ole days in South Florida; they are held close in those memories and thankfully, being kept amongst old friends and acquaintances via social media.

I began this piece on a delightful Valentine's Day morning in 2018 with the intention of writing a bit of nostalgia and then directing my thoughts and words towards the imminent approaching of spring, but then, the Florida school shooting happened before I finished this piece. Coincidentally, I was writing about the idyllic childhood experiences of my husband who grew up in that area and now, my mind is instead tainted with what just occurred. It reminded me of the feeling I felt when Nice, France was involved in the massacre on Bastille Day two summers ago. Nice was a beautiful place from my youth that had suddenly become tarnished and toxic from the unthinkable crime committed there. Anyway, with the developing news blaring from the TV on channels 5 to a zillion, it became difficult to write about the coming of spring and hearts and flowers amongst the intensity of pain that was, is, occurring. How did we get to this place?

March 2018

The fields are yellow, my sister, Susan's, favorite color. I find joy looking at nature's spring bouquet and I am happy for my bees to feast on the nectar and the birds to scatter the seeds. It is all a pleasant display of new life. I write this with words from the heart and feelings that have recently been amplified by sorrow. For those of you who know me, you know about the cut that indiscriminately and suddenly sliced through my world just last week, a wound that is deep and everlasting, the loss of a precious sister.

Spring, this year offers a special meaning to me as I travel forth in this new dimension of life, a place without someone I love. It is a dimension we all visit at some point, the dimension of loss, the dimension that forces us to be very human and vulnerable, the dimension that reminds us that life is fleeting.

I have not been able to find much of a muse these past few days; I am "borrowing" a happy little blog post of mine from many years ago. I hope you enjoy it.

"I was outside early one morning last week, a morning before the rains came when late spring and hints of summer were intermingling. I was in my garden picking strawberries I had planted in November – trying to beat the birds, breaking the fast of the night – it was wonderful, pure, whole food from my backyard. I have to say, growing your own food is fulfilling. I suppose the cultivation deed is somewhere in our DNA – a survival tool that we are hard wired for. I heard yesterday that one component of well-being and good health is to have something to look forward to. Growing your food gives that to you along with whole food that is free from chemicals and filled with nutrients. Just a small patch of land can do big things for your health. Just saying...

Later, while in the woods, I was dazzled once again by the cobwebs that extended over the paths - masterpieces in the early mornings with dew outlining their shapes and emphasizing their details - little Rembrandts of the night reminding me of chalk artist in today's cities - working so hard to create, only to be dissolved by an inevitable looming force of nature.

The day rolls out like a tapestry rug - each hour offering something different than the one before, like the chapters of our lives, unfolding and delivering little pieces of art that delight us and then disappear into the morning light of the next day where, if we look ahead, we will see yet another masterpiece beginning.

Anyway…this is my little post of the week. I hope you can find something worthwhile within this pile of thoughts that became words and perhaps push you to make certain you have something to look forward to, whether it is a child coming home for a visit or a trip you may take or a ripe strawberry in your backyard."

I end with a reminder that the Full Sap Moon will rise on the 31st. It will be the second full moon this month, hence, a Blue Moon. Spring will be delivered this Tuesday and Passover and Easter will soon follow. The Earth is, once again, waking up from the slumber of winter and offering all of us a new beginning. Take it.

April 2018

I sat at the open bridge in Morbihan one recent day, while a tugboat towed down the bayou. I knew it would be a while, so I did not resist. I put the windows down, turned off the radio, and listened. I fell back into another time, a time before the "new" 1966 bridge was built, a time when Morbihan was a quiet little community somewhat secretly nestled along the Teche where everyone knew everyone else, and many were related and had never left. The Conrad's lived there. Mrs. Conrad gave me my first art lesson at her kitchen table; a portrait of Spencer Tracy as Hemingway's old man in the sea. It was a lesson in oils; I had never heard of acrylic paint then – oils were exclusive and wonderful (they still are). There was a bridge keeper there also. His tiny house was near the bridge, somewhat shielded by a mature fig tree. It was very quiet then and there; hardly anyone lived out here, the Cajun Coop was not built yet, and there was no Emile Verret Road. Instead, there was an old wooden store sitting in the exact spot that currently begins this, now, much traveled road.

This memory was from a long time ago when the world was big and still and unobtrusive. Something as simple as going to the old store for a grape corn sucker was eventful and sitting in a car at night with the windows rolled down in the middle of nowhere (without a cell phone) waiting for the bridge to close was safe. I would listen to the sounds coming from the bayou and perhaps hear a faraway freight train, never fearing anything in the dark stillness of the country, hearing only peaceful noises from the natural world as I sat snuggly in the backseat of our car and waited to cross over. Anyway, I sat there for a while and the soothing breeze and the sound of the tugboat helped me to remember that time, that time when my thoughts were original and not spiked with clamor and endless propaganda and my world was safe.

The world is very busy now. Information comes at us even when we try to hide, too much information, much of it useless and meant only to provoke, that's what I think. I threaten, at least once a week, to disconnect, to go back to how things were just a decade ago but then, I don't; I don't think we can anymore. It was Darwin that said, "It is not the strongest or the most intelligent who will survive but those who can best manage change." I might be doomed.

These days of spring are sudden and so sweet. The air is filled with frolic and fragrance and a certain sense of renewal and optimism. Just this morning, I noticed the Ligustrum trumping the light fragrance of the mimosa and bright yellow irises peeking out from dense green leaves, still a bit timid, but about to be fabulous. The birds are back and flying overhead in glorious formations and are singing sweetly to wake me up. The honeybees are busy pollinating my garden and cleaning their little feet in the bird bath when they return from their long day of foraging and the moon is new. It is truly an awakening, so beautiful and divine. I cannot stay inside in Spring. My house does suffer a bit from neglect when the calendar turns to April and May. It is somewhat "clean", but not fussy. The dishes are washed and stacked neatly on the little rack next to the sink, the bed has been made, the bathrooms scrubbed, and the laundry hung out to dry – I say, enough is done. The focus is on the outside beauty. Cut gardenias will soon be in jars in the kitchen, the screen door will be left open filling the den with the smell of honeysuckle, and a special friend, a beautiful person has a birthday today; these are the things that matter to me. These are the things that never change.

May 2018

It is Sunday, the Sunday before Mother's Day, the Sunday before you read this. I am in my kitchen cleaning up from breakfast and somewhat mindlessly planning tonight's supper. I have brown rice from yesterday (too much to give to my chickens), a freezer full of vegetables and a basket of red onions. That would be a fine beginning coupled with a honey dew that is sitting on my countertop continuing to ripen.

A small bouquet of Gardenias that I picked late yesterday afternoon still scents a small place in the kitchen and there is a quart of blackberries waiting for more shortcake in my refrigerator. In my somewhat contemplative state, I watch from the window as 3 playful squirrels raid my bird feeder and a male and female cardinal wait for and then feed on the muddle the squirrels are making.

As I watch them eat and romp, I drift into thoughts of my sister, Susan, something I do many times throughout my day. It is Sunday, so we would not have talked on the phone until later today. She would be busy in her kitchen preparing some wonderful meal for her family. It was something my mother did, and she carried on, Sunday dinner. She was the keeper of those types of traditions; that was her joy and her homage to our mother.

From there, my thoughts lengthen; I think of all mothers and the unending day work we do, work that comes undone by nightfall. I think of the laundry, the shopping, the cooking, the mending, and the tending all bundled up to make our houses into homes. The rewards, for the most part, are not very tangible; singularly, they are faint and obscure but cumulatively, they become the fabric of our families and carve a place in the hearts of our children, a place that will, hopefully, remain. My mother and my sister did this; I strive to.

As a few of you know, I keep bees. Because of this, I know that "the flow" is at its height now. This is a special time in spring when the most flowers are blooming. Right now, on this day, our world is filled with maximum color and fragrance and our sky is filled with enchantment. The Full Flower Moon will rise on the 29th and if you look into the eastern sky around nightfall, you will see Jupiter, not to be mistaken for Venus which hangs brightly, brighter than Jupiter, in the western sky sometime after sunset. Treat yourself and take it in.

To all the mothers reading this, I hope you find happiness within your day and that you always cherish the life you are living and the many moments you are unselfishly giving; it matters.

June 2018

Storms are moving into Acadiana as I put this piece together. I welcome them. The first week of June is here and soon the heat will linger and the locusts will chirp at sunset and the time will slow down just a bit as the days lengthen and nightfall finds us tired from the heat and the garden. There are six blushing tomatoes on my windowsill, sliced cucumbers in the refrigerator and yellow squash scattered on my kitchen counter. Sunflowers are hovering above the immature okra plants in my garden and the smell of honey scents my bee yard; the first month of summer is in full bloom.

Earlier this week, I spent a hot summer morning in my chicken yard; the hens watched me from their coops like a baby watches its mother as she walks across the room. The heat was intense; I wanted to feel it because, with it, came secrets of summer - I saw green dragonflies lighting on colorful zinnias, lime green lizards hunting for lunch, and in the silence of the morning, I heard birds calling out to one another and a single squirrel rustling in a faraway tree as I turned over the soil to plant a persimmon tree within the boundaries of what used to be Elizabeth's butterfly garden.

Matthew recently noticed that I am 'pulling in'. I am. I have years of growth in the nearby field, fruit trees and berries and a vegetable garden, but it will become a long journey to there if I am here as a very old woman. So, in case, I am pulling in. My bees and chickens are already near. Now, I am like Noah, planting one of each kind of fruit tree nearby.

I read the recent headlines. I know things are changing here, people moving out, crime moving in. I cannot complain because I have no solution to offer and my children are included in those numbers that have moved away, job opportunities directed them. But I am just like many others; I want to stay here. We have spent nearly a lifetime rooting ourselves. Amongst the noise, I do feel some encouragement within the community now and then. The other day, Matt, Drew, and I went to the Fresh Market on Hopkins searching for produce for our restaurant and we spent time with someone who radiates positive energy and gives me hope, Carl Patrick Cooper Jr. He has taken an unassuming spot and vacant lot on Hopkins Street and is transforming it into a vision.

Sometime in 2013, he had an "aha" moment that reconnected him to his heritage and his culture. He resolutely changed his life and his diet and began a journey of self-awareness and health. He trusted his decision to follow a new path and, with uncertainty, but with much determination, he made the effort. In 2015, he was introduced to Phanat and Envision Da Berry by a friend and elderly entrepreneur, Mr. Rudolph Plomboy, who also had a business in the Westend, The House of Rudolph...and his vision took shape.

What follows are Carl's words and what I see as his mission statement..."Working hard to make more progressive changes and connections in the community... Breaking through toxic barriers that needed to be broken and learning the truth behind miseducation. I'm diligently working towards growing and developing Da Berry Fresh Market to become prosperous, self-sufficient, and job creating. While giving back in numerous ways to help revive, heal, and empower a torn and broken community, I intend to give others natural healthy fresh options along with a very pleasant new experience."

I applaud him and I look forward to his success and to possibly more of our youth finding ways to make New Iberia a wonderful place to live.

I conclude with a pleasant reminder, the first day of summer is on the 21st and the Full Strawberry Moon is on the 28th, and a wish that you have homegrown tomatoes on your supper table and green dragonflies on your zinnias.

July 2018

I was born on the fourth of July. At least I was supposed to, but I came early, I was born on June 29. Pretty close prediction of due date considering the year 1954. Imagine no sonograms or technology to make that determination, just some numbers and a doctor who was more than likely just my mom's family doctor.

I am writing this on the Fourth of July, I like to let you know when I write because it does play a part in what I write, it helps to bring you into the story a bit more.

There aren't many firecrackers popping this morning, the time and rain has taken care of that.

We did not fire up the grill and we have no Roman Candles to send off or sparklers to make circles in the darkness with, those days are somewhat behind us now. I still enjoy the thought of it all, but I must admit, I do love the peace of the present.

I will cut open a fat watermelon and cut okra. I will wait until night to swim and watch the sky light up with fireworks from the next neighborhood and look for Saturn and Venus holding still in the summer sky, then it will be the 4th of July.

August 2018

The skies are rumbling right now, reminding me of awaiting autumn storms and the season shifting. It is Tuesday morning, and I can only think of a family today that is having to endure such a deep and sudden loss, a family that becomes our family when hurt like this happens. I write this but there is nothing I can say. I only feel.

The month will soon be over, another summer will be gone and whatever happened or did not happen is of no matter now. September, we are ready; I suppose. I know retail and consumerism will soon, if not already, be unleashed and some will begin to feel the intense pressure that is frantically pumped in through the wires or through the wireless wonders, whichever. I, for one, will take Robert Frost's Road Less Traveled and follow Henry David Thoreau into the woods. I will have very little to do with the commercialism that is about to be upon us citizens of the world.

In the field near my garden this morning, I watched a bird, before the storm. She was feeling some stress herself; I think. The clouds were moving fast, and the noise of the thunder was distant but elevating and approaching. She flew from tree to tree trying to find that safe place to be, a place to shield herself from the oncoming storm. I will do as that bird and search to find a place away from the storm, a place within nature where things are real and warm, the way I want the upcoming holiday season to be, for me.

But, before all of that, there will be the harvest. The mill will be turned on once again, the festival will come to town and while looking so cultural and quaint, the filled-up tractors will "challenge" our patience on the back roads. This is so much a part of our town and like life itself, it offers a myriad of hometown feelings.

I, for one, love the celebration of harvest. I live amongst the rural fields near Loreauville, and I see the farmers in their fields and on their tractors, working in the very early morning, beneath the powerful summer sun. They and the people they hire are tending the crops that is their livelihood, continuing in families, staying close to the earth, doing what we have done since our country began, planting and harvesting. I wish all our farmers a safe and bountiful harvest...

The Full Harvest Moon will be September 24 this year. As I always write to remind, the Harvest Moon can either be in September or October, depending on proximity to the Autumnal Equinox. It is a wonderful time of year, a time to take out the gumbo pots, plant cruciferous vegetables, and look ahead with wonderment as the season changes and we enjoy the bounty of the good earth.

I end this somewhat ambiguous piece with the same sentiment I began with. I, like everyone in this compassionate community, am thinking of the families that are feeling the very new and raw pain of loss, a pain common, in varying degrees, to all of mankind. Clearly, I cannot remove the hurt, all I can do is offer heartfelt sympathy and my belief that your love lives on.

September 28, 2018

When I was growing up, there were places I had (big) ideas about, dreams about, really. I would drive through the alley next to Kings Office Supply and the Masonic Building and imagine the little building facing the alley to be my art studio, someday. I would drive out of town on the Weeks Island Road and go to Mrs. Ella Kean's house to talk about art and to see her paintings that were scattered throughout her house, huge paintings of pink flowers and bold impressionistic expressions. I remember her telling my mom that, after high school, I should go, had to go to, to New York City to an art school. Well, that would be, then, like going on a moon ride now. My parents could not afford such an education and besides, New York City was worlds and worlds away; Baton Rouge would be the furthest I could venture.

There was no I10 in the summer of 1972, instead, getting to school was a long trek through Krotz Springs and bottle necks along the way; Baton Rouge was far far away.

Art and Nature were my focuses in life then. I consumed all the information I could find, I read *Lust for Life* and *Walden Pond* and somehow managed to convince my parents, in my junior year at LSU, that I needed to study in southern France, to be amongst Van Gogh's cypress trees and to sit near the sea. I did that and I painted with oils and a palette knife, and I kept journals with nature drawings, and I ate tarts and drank just a bit of Bordeaux. I have carried those moments with me throughout my life, always appreciating the sacrifice my parents made to give me these rich experiences and their origins along the Teche.

Here I am now...I am 64 and have visited Thoreau's Walden Pond in the summer of 2012 and have returned to southern France in 2017, those places that held magic for me as a young girl. I saw them differently, I saw them as beautiful but not as magical; that is something sheltered in youth, the magic. There always exist the mystical and spiritual aspects of life from the miracle of birth until the transition of death, but the magic of youth is some of the best stuff, the stuff that is brilliant and, seemingly, all possible.

I write this as somewhat of a lament. I write and wonder if those places of enchantment still exist within our town for our youth. I hope so. I hope there are places within that are still inspiring the children of New Iberia, places that spark imagination and interest, places that may be the catalyst to lead them in a direction that they build their lives around. I hope we can still offer that. I was so fulfilled as a young girl growing up here. There were so many interesting places and people that inspired me, places like Sr Ann Carmel's art class and Mrs. Ella's house that smell of turpentine and was filled with encouragement. I have never forgotten those feelings of inspiration; I have never forgotten the "magic" I found in my hometown.

October 2018

I am stopping to write. It is Wednesday. The Full Hunter Moon will rise tonight, whether I can see it or not, it will be there. I am not a hunter; I suppose I would be considered more of a gatherer, but I do understand and respect the importance of this moon long ago when supermarkets did not dot this land and hunters, men I suppose, had to find food to eat and share with their families and neighbors; this moon was of great assistance. I honor it still.

I did not feel much like putting a piece together today, only because I have little of interest to say to you. By choice, I have settled into a very simple routine, I seldom go anywhere socially. I am always happy to run into new and old friends at the grocery store or at Caribbean Ice – my two excursions – I just have less interest in "getting out", therefore, little to report in that regard. Right now, this computer that I am using to write my column, there is nothing 'on' in my house. The TV is off, no music is playing, my phone is quiet, as it updates, and the landline is mute. The silencing of these things has created this environment that once was a part all our lives, a place of stillness and a place where you listened to your thoughts and formed your opinions (and wrote your column).

Within this realm of peacefulness, I decided to clean out my purse, a fun bohemian bag I bought at a market in San Antonio this spring when Skip and I were on a visit to see William and Lorena. I carefully emptied it on the keeping room table and found a spilled bottle of Tylenol, lipstick, a broken ball point pen and an assortment of old receipts. There was no sound in my house, just me and the little task at hand. I thought about me, I thought about how I was feeling and sort of got reacquainted with myself digging through the history of this purse and the trail it left while sitting in silence on this autumn day of the Hunters Moon. I realized how powerful and nurturing this silence was and, sadly, how elusive it has become in today's world, a world too many times crowded with ego driven toxic shouts across the boundless airwaves. I also thought about young people and wondered where do they go to get away from the noise, where do they go to hear their own unique voices and to discover who they (really) are?

I made a small "to do list" this morning …strawberries, pansies and a banana plant to plant, roast a chicken with some of the rosemary I have growing at Caribbean Ice and fill and send a package to Elizabeth on Cape Cod, just some fun things like a Halloween ribbon for her hair, some warm stockings for winter and a scattering of heartfelt words on a card. I think I will get this all done. These tasks are the fluff to enjoy amongst all that must be done today, all the day work, the work we all must tend to.

Amongst the fleeting stillness of my morning, I walked outside and picked a few persimmons, spotted a late season monarch caterpillar on a milkweed plant, and happily picked two eggs from my pullets…highlights for me in this 64th year, in this place in life that wants more stillness than stimulation, a peaceful place to write this "Seinfeldish" Sunday column.

November 2018

The birds aren't here yet. And some people aren't here either, the people of Christmas past. We all know them; we all miss them. For me, this year, it is my sister, Susan, that I will miss most. I was 4 when she was born and since then I have never shared Christmas without her. From the days of the matching Christmas dresses my grandmother Farris made and wishes from the Sears and Roebuck Christmas Book, to waking up our parents at 4 am Christmas morning and all those magical moments in between and beyond, I will miss her until it hurts.

As I plant a pear tree, long before Arbor Day, I find the little slugs in the ground already bedded down for the winter and I know the caterpillars are snuggled in piles of leaves and the Canadian geese are once again sitting on the banks of the Hudson. The squirrels outside of the kitchen window rush each morning to gather acorns just as they have always done, and the bees are much fewer now and not as busy for they have their pantry filled with enough honey to last the winter. All nature is finding its place during these milder days before Christmas. I too shall find mine, once again. There will be someone missing beneath the tree, they are still here however, they have just moved.

Have a wonderful holiday with those that are here, while keeping the memories from Christmas past.

December 23, 2018

I walked through the house very early this morning before lights were turned on, before coffee was made, and before the day began. The scattered strands of Christmas lights lit the way. Everything was still in the empty rooms; I could feel the history there – the babies, the birthday parties, my mom's little visits, my dad sitting on the kitchen chair, Christmases past, it was all there in the quietness amongst the twinkling lights.

It was a lonely feeling but somehow welcome, this visitor from Christmas past, the one I wrote of last month, he came. Christmas present is here, right here, right now. My four sons have all found their way home for a short, but cherished visit. My daughter will not, she is far away, but she is happy, so I am too.

This day, December 21, begins the Winter Solstice, the one day a year when our shadows at noon are the longest. The Full Cold Moon will rise tomorrow, the 22nd, - hopefully in a clear, cold winter sky. I find opportunity for reflection and renewal in winter as I watch how Nature sheds her luster and her protection so nobly – how she is brought to her bare bones and survives it, she gets through it only to reintroduce herself in spring. She does this each year. I suppose this is some kind of cleansing, a purging that is necessary to grow and, because of my beliefs,

I feel it is something I should follow – unlike man's decrees; Nature's laws are consistent and non-discriminate. So, I begin this winter with that in mind – the season to purge – both my thoughts and my things and in spring I hope I have looked within and am ready for the awakening of another opportunity to bloom.

I wish you pure and pronounced moments during this holiday season that will become soothing memories in the years to come – moments that find you outside looking at the Christmas sky, moments that include hugs and warm smiles and moments that find you alone in a cozy chair stopping to think about yourself and what is really important while welcoming this starkness that is winter. For it is this nakedness, that allows us to find some answers exposed there against the bareness and beauty that is Nature.

Make a cup of hot cocoa and enjoy this, the coldest season, the season to tuck in, reflect and restore.

Happy Christmas.

January 2019

I've heard somewhere that we should move every 10 years to avoid excessive accumulation. If that is true, I am 25 years overdue. It is January and I am being assaulted with messages that we need to clean out things...our closets, our emails, our refrigerators, and our lives; we need less stuff so we can have more time.

It is, I think, a good suggestion, so, I am making a colossal try to comply. I have even watched Marie Kondo on Netflix a couple of times for inspiration. However, I am still a bit overwhelmed with the tough task of filtering through my life here on Vida Shaw Road, in a house that we built in 1984, a place where we raised our children, a place where so much happened and the physical manifestations are everywhere. It is that house with an attic filled with dinosaurs, superheroes, and American Girls. It is the house that keeps the memories safe in shoe boxes stacked in closets and hidden in the dark corners of cabinets, the house that still has white polished high-top shoes from Babineaux's and Denby Stoneware from Abdalla's gift shop and a few Big Chief tablets from Howard Brothers. There are even colorful magnetic refrigerator letters in a candy jar, A to Z. What do we do with all these things that we have scribed our memories into, these things that are the bread crumb trails to our yesterdays?

I type and think as this stream of conscious musing manifests near the end of this month of January, this month where many resolutions have already become diluted. I am determined to accomplish much of my goal, I will filter so that I can, as promised, experience the freedom of less.

In opposition to all the above, however, one of the sweetest memories I have of my parents' house was found in the little forgotten cabinet above the kitchen sink. I discovered it when we were going through everything after my mom died. It was THE medicine cabinet. Behind the tiny birch doors was all a mother in the 60s needed to raise healthy children to adulthood...a bottle of Creomulsion for our coughs, a thermometer to tell if we had fever, a bottle of St. Joseph Baby Aspirin if we did, an opaque jar of Vicks Vapor Rub for chest congestion, a small bottle of Mercurochrome or the dreaded Merthiolate for our cuts and scrapes, and Pepto Bismol that, she said, tasted like bubble gum, for our upset stomachs. That was it. Of course, everything in this little time capsule was "tossed", but my short journey was warm, and I have kept it always.

I know that the "things" are not the memory, but the "things" awaken it. I have no conclusion to offer concerning this fumbling thought of simplifying. I suppose I will land somewhere in the middle of this heap of "things". I will "toss" and I will "keep" and if I ever move, I will be forced to "toss" some more.

Amid this clean up conundrum, I took a break and walked around the yard and into the woods. Both were seemingly barren until I stopped and looked beneath; there were worlds of motion and life spinning throughout the winter landscape; tiny forms of existence were scurrying and nesting and moving things around, the squirrels were terribly busy finding food and shelter, the sky was sometimes darkened with hawks hunting;

Nature never really sleeps. She is most always busy, preparing food, cleaning nests, moving, redefining, always a schedule to keep and housekeeping to do. We too have schedules to keep and "housekeeping" to tend to; Nature gives us winter to go beneath and sort and clean and 'toss'. I will do as she does, but I will leave a few breadcrumbs to find my way home.

February 2019

I wear an apron most days. Not just for cooking and baking, like you may expect, but for painting – for art. I passed by a mirror just now and saw myself in one, the little royal blue one with a row of pockets, and I quickly remembered the aprons from my childhood, icons of the 60s "housewife". The pockets were usually trimmed with scrap pieces of Rik Rak and filled with small household items picked up along the ways of her day and sorted through at the end of it, when it then hung on a hook near the kitchen, waiting for duty the next morning, ready to, once again, shield the splatters of her day.

My grandmother, my dad's mom, had beautiful aprons that she made with scrap pieces of fabric, Rik Rak, and colorful buttons – they were always there protecting her homemade dress from chicken frying and whirls of all-purpose flour. My mamae, my mom's mother, wore aprons too. I don't know if she made hers, but they competently took her through her days in the kitchen just the same, baking sweet tarts and cooking couvillions.

My own mother wore an apron also, mostly on Thanksgiving and Easter, protecting holiday clothes from cheese sauces and turkey basting. I have a vision of her in her apron, an image that says "mother". There were clothespins, bobby pins, banana magnolia pods, or just something she might need in the pockets of her apron, but always, it was an expression of home.

I wear one now for painting, gardening and, of course, for cooking. When I do, I love that it becomes a little toolbox for me – collecting things in the pockets, things I need or squirrelling small things I find in the house that belong somewhere else, wiping wet hands with its skirt, gathering eggs, stashing empty seed packets, and feeling reflective in it, wondering why I don't include it in my day more often. But, like so many other household icons – the apron may be disappearing with diaper pins and Simplicity patterns.

It appears the groundhog may have been right; spring seems to be peeping around the brief and windy wall of winter. My fruit trees are beginning to bud and the field is covered with yellow wildflowers. I have heard the mating calls of the robins so I will begin to look for their nests in unusual places, in my old garden shed, boots that were left outside or some place that has not been disturbed for a while; they don't seem to mind being near people. This makes me happy because spotting a blue robin egg is one of the most wonderful things to discover.

There will be a full moon on the 20th of March, the first day of Spring. This moon is named the Full Worm Moon, it will be a the last of the three consecutive supermoons. I hope it will be a crystal-clear night that will have concluded a beautiful spring day, one filled with mating calls of early spring and thoughts of apron strings from long ago.

March 2019

This piece is a reflection about a seemingly ordinary kitchen window and an old clock, both about the same age, both a part of my home.

I've looked out of this kitchen window for 34 years. I've watched little boys learn to ride bikes without training wheels, while their dad ran alongside ready to catch them before they fell and I've watched grown up boys drive up from faraway places, home for a visit. I've watched a "princess" leave for her first overnight birthday party with a tiara and a Barbie bag and return from high school in a VW with the radio turned up too loud. I've seen my mom pull up in the early morning for a quick cup of coffee and, without knowing, watched her drive away for the last time. I have watched my dad in his blue Crown Vic driving over for a late afternoon visit, just to get out of the house when my mom was no longer there. I've watched trees grow and our dog run through the yard and my chickens peck and squirrels and robins and neighbors walking. I have lined baby bottles along its sill to dry and I have cleaned it a thousand times.

I have seen much life through this kitchen window. Each day I am anxious to look through it and watch what passes by. I await the show, this display of life. I make myself remember the small but most precious moments within those years and the joy from the people I have watched through this familiar glass.

Now, mostly, I watch the wildlife. I have a birdfeeder that I keep filled with seed and our trees are now mature and filled with acorns so the squirrels have made homes here. I hear them in the early morning scrambling across the roof and onto the treetops wondering what the hurry is. I usually see the first hummingbird of the season through this window, and I watch as the first cold front rolls in. It is a cozy view of the world.

Thirty-four years ago, I ordered a wall clock from the Spiegel catalogue. It told time and chimed to remind me that it would soon be evening, and my husband would be home, and the kids would be more settled. It has been silent for so many years – silent because I eventually had no time to wind it, no time for it to tell me what time it was – it didn't seem to matter then, it was just time – something I had plenty of. I was too busy, so busy, pushing through the channels of my life – quickly and many times without notice. Now, at 64, I think of winding it again, this old clock from a place that does not exist anymore. I could, now, listen to what it has to say, I would listen to each tick it makes and know that this is my life these minutes and seconds I hear in this house that is quieter now. I am aware of the time in my day, and I am more careful with it as I wait for more to come, more life to see from my kitchen window.

April 2019

This April day ends with a few small kitchen chores…putting away a few dishes, wiping the crumbs from the cabinet space near the toaster, popping lids back on spice bottles and almond cans and pulling the little lace kitchen window curtains together.

While putting away some extra-large salad bowls in the cabinet beneath the candles, I met with some obstacles – a messy and out of order condition within the cupboard that kept me from stacking an oversized red bowl. I decided that "now" was a good time to straighten it up a bit. I reached in to take out everything (just a soon wipe the shelf down while reorganizing) and saw something from long ago hiding in the corner. It was a juicer – not one like my mom used, the glass one that required squeezing an orange half over its pointed protrusion, this one was electric – simple, but electric; it was mine.

I instantly thought of summer days long ago when boredom was lurking, and kids were little and twitchy as the minutes sometimes crawled. Luckily, I had always kept a few things in my bag of tricks to cure monotony, one was the performance of this dutiful device. I would take out a sack of oranges and this fancy juicer and some little fellows would take turns juicing. I had a little wooden stool to scoot up against the cabinet and their chucky little legs would hang from the seat as they had their turn turning navel oranges into a summer brew. The time passed, the oranges juiced, the rinds went into the compost bowl and the boredom was dispersed.

When I saw that old appliance in the corner of the cupboard, I went back "there" so quickly. Back to a summer afternoon with little boys looking for something to do and the solution being so simple – just a distraction to reroute the afternoon.

Now, a professional Vita Mixer has a place of honor on my kitchen cabinet and nearly every morning I make green smoothies. While spinach and whatever fresh and/or frozen fruit I have, go into the big and powerful Vita Mixer and a glass of very nutritious juice suddenly appears, the journey is not key here – there will be no moments to remember, just juice to drink. There is no lifting little boys up on wooden stools to reach the old juicer that mesmerized and entertained on a long summer afternoon in the country. It now sits still in a dark corner of my kitchen cabinet hardly remembered and never used.

There is also a little guy in the corner on the top shelf of my spice cabinet. He has curious eyes and cinnamon smudges on his face, sitting there since 1985! I cleaned out my little spice cabinet yesterday and, once again, I dusted him off and put him back in his corner. I'll take him out again around Christmas – one morning when it's cold and it's Saturday and time for hot chocolate and cinnamon toast.

I don't really know why I hang on to and refill such a peculiar inanimate object – something from Winn Dixie that I bought when my oldest boys were about 3 or 4. Anyway, there he was again, sitting still with his red cap, waiting and causing me to reel backwards into what I remember to be such a wonderful time – a time of youth, both mine and my children's, a time when I had my parents there to cushion the blows and filter the toxins of my life, a time when tomorrow was stretched out into infinity, it seemed. Maybe that is why "he" sits there in my spice cabinet with his quirky smile and his twist top cap…to remind me of the moments that matter.

May 2019

The room, my studio, is quiet now, the radio turned to classic country is silent, the caps are on the tubes of paint, the memories are doused, and the lights are off, it's only the early morning rays that move about giving some illumination and hint to the night before – Saturday night is over. There is some song about how everything looks different in the morning light. It does.

Sometimes, on Saturday nights, I listen to old country from 6 to midnight and I paint. It is when I allow myself to go back in time to drench myself in melancholia and think of the people from long ago. It is a ritual, my muse; it is a way to create, a way to tap into something way beneath the surface; old memories make it happen.

I wake up on Sunday mornings and walk in my quiet studio and there on the easel are tangibles from the night before – it is wonderful for me. It's the music, the solitude, and the distance from obligation (and sometimes a few tears) that gets me there.

I remember, sometimes, on Saturday afternoons, my mom would listen to music on the radio, and she would cry. I was young then and my past was short and unblemished; I did not understand her tears, tears that would just seemingly show up. I do now, I understand those thoughts of yesterday that well up your eyes and take possession of your heart, those times and people in your life that are gone, at least gone from this physical world. And I understand that music, especially old songs, are a stimulus for these moments. I also know that those moments are necessary and somehow healing, at least for me.

Memories are pulled from us by songs and visuals and even fragrances and every now and then we need to visit those places. When I do, I learn something, I reflect and I think of things my mother said or did and it fits into my life now and I "get it", I "get" her. It's as though her life remains a part of mine – she is still my teacher, my role model, my mother, and the thousands of words she spoke, the timeless thoughts she shared, the unconditional love she gave me are all still here and each day, I use some of those treasures she has left for me.

My mother-in-law once gave me some very valuable advice about moms telling their children things they feel they should know – she told me to keep talking to my kids, no matter if it didn't seem as though they were listening – just keep filling their heads with the right stuff and someday, somewhere they will draw from my words. I have found this to be some of the best parenting advice ever. Thank you, Molly Shensky.

Anyway, it is Sunday morning now and the muse is gone with the rising sun. I hope somewhere in this entry you can find something to relate to and to encourage you to set aside time to reflect and to cry and to feel all those things that living provides you with. For me, it's important to have those moments that take me back to those days and those people that helped to bring me to this point in my life. It takes quiet time to "go there" – it takes music, a book, a sky full of stars or a blank canvas and a country song.

Happy Mother's Day to all...keep talking to your children, no matter how old they are; one day, it will all be understood.

June 2019

An excerpt from my blog written years ago..

I am in my "summer" house now, now that May is gone. The blinds are open just like always but now, in this "summer" house, the light comes in at a different slant and dances over my paintings and our harvest table with more enthusiasm and delight. The yard in summer speaks a different language also. The birds have returned from their long journey across the Gulf of Mexico, and they reconnect to one another with loud and boisterous sounds when the heat is at its highest in the middle of the day and in the morning, they exchange gentle chirps and melodies that wake me. At night, in the summer yard, there are tree frogs sounding away their thoughts and needs throughout the dusk and are silenced only by the distant howling of coyotes and the nearby rustling of raccoons in limbs all looking keenly for food. I haven't heard the cicadas, the ice cream truck, or the mosquito truck yet, those sounds will wait and come deeper in summer.

For now, I will enjoy the delicate light through my keeping room window in the late afternoon, pick blackberries in the early morning beating the birds and the heat, cut early blooming zinnias to put in Elizabeth's clay pots and enjoy these effervescent moments in my "summer" house.

This summer will be my 65th summer of this life. I reflect about how much I have seen and how little I know. I think of the lives before me and how they accumulated knowledge and passed it on and I wonder how we don't know everything by now, why don't we learn, why don't we listen?

It really all seems to stay the same, we really are no different than those who lived before, only the costumes and props have changed. As I write this, I think, maybe this is how it should be, maybe we all must take the same journey again and again, maybe that's life. If so, perhaps we should just enjoy this gift and not look so intensely for the answers, for even if they are found, many times we don't learn.

Many of the answers we need have been discovered anyway. We all know that love is the most important and beneficial emotion we have and yet we still witness hate each day of our lives, we all know that money cannot buy lasting happiness yet we all watch and sometimes partake in the intense and sometimes corrupt pursuit of it, we know that wars do not bring about lasting peace but we still fight, we know that we all are fighting the same battles yet we still hurt and humiliate each other, we all know that overeating makes us fat yet we are the weightiest ever, and we know that children need love and guidance but so many are denied either. It seems we should be so shrewd by now; we should have life figured out by now.

I think these thoughts as I approach 65 and, like you, scratch my head and try to understand but, like all that have come before, I will not fully know why. So, I write about the honeybees that I watch each day and find solace in their routine and their predictable pattern that they have followed forever. I find joy discovering the first dragonfly of summer and the discovery of bluebirds in the handmade box that faces the field and I wait for the full moon every 28 nights, for these things are real and these things show me that life is a continuous cycle that certainly includes us, tenacious as we may sometimes be.

I will spend my day doing many things, many tasks that need to be done, but I will wait for the late afternoon sun to spill into my kitchen and assure me that life goes on as it always has and I will, for that moment, feel a part of it and I will be happy in my "summer" house.

July 2019

I hang on to the small rituals of the day, I hang on because they are, in this world of uncertainty, the things I can be sure of. I am happy to be in this somewhat bucolic space, this is the place I am used to, the place I know so well; it is home. I know that the mockingbirds live in the white oak near the garden shed. I sometimes watch helplessly as they scare away the tiny Bluebirds in early Spring and raid my biggest fig tree each July morning. I know that there is a green lizard that lives behind the wooden shutter of my kitchen window, and he comes out into the sun while I am making coffee each morning in summer. I watch him and he watches me. He puffs up and scurries upward and away from my view after a few moments of "eye" contact, as if to say, rather gruffly and grumpily, "good morning".

I know that the tree frogs sing with the moon rising and that my honeybees are collecting at the opening of the hive, feverishly fanning to keep things bearable inside for their queen and her brood. I know that I may have picked the last magnolia and that this midsummer heat is for my zinnias and lantana; the gentle bloom of summer has passed, and the temperature is not kind to many of my other flowers.

But I will embrace you, this seventh month, the hottest month. I will listen to you when you suggest I wake up very early to do the outside things, to water the flowers and pick the figs. I will listen when you suggest I spend the hot afternoons inside, knowing, that later, I will be able to enjoy your gentle evenings as the locusts holler, the fireflies quietly blink amongst the trees, and the katydids chirp, seemingly saying, in the balmy night air, "Katy did" and then answering with "Katy didn't".

Now and then, I may find a late blooming magnolia and catch a trace of its lemon fragrance and I will, now, enjoy the full bloom of the Crepe Myrtles as this lovely season of summer proceeds. I will join the chorus of all that I meet as we begin each conversation with "It's hot", a perpetual southern "complaint" spoken by all, for all time. It is something so expected. I will have slices of cold watermelon in my refrigerator, ice in all my tea and plenty of water for my plants and animals. It is time to be hot, it is July. Just as I am submitting to the overgrowth from the woods and to the abundance of sapling sprouts in my yard, I am submitting to the heat. It is how our world turns.

The dog days of summer began July 3 and will end on August 11. The dog star, Sirius, will rise at dawn. These will be the hottest days of summer...get ready. The full moon will be on the 16th and it will be the Full Buck Moon. I understand that long long ago, the Indians gave it this name because it is the time of year when the antlers begin to push through the foreheads of the deer, the buck deer. I also have heard it called the Full Thunder Moon because of the volatile storms of midsummer. Either way, I hope the sky is clear on the 16th so we can have a remarkable view of it.

Hurricane season is upon us, enjoy your lovely yards during these days of quietness, for, as we all know too well, our enchanting Gulf can churn and then turn against us becoming explosive and reminding us that Mother

Nature is, and should be, still in charge.
Stay cool and find the fireflies.

August 2019

I sat at the open bridge in Morbihan one recent day, as a tugboat was towing down the bayou. I knew it would be a while, so, I did not resist. I put the windows down, turned off the radio and listened. I fell back into another time, a time before the "new" 1966 bridge was built, a time when Morbihan was a quiet little community nestled along the Teche where everyone knew everyone else, and many were related and had never left.

The Conrad's lived there. Mrs. Conrad gave me my first art lesson at her kitchen table; a portrait of Spencer Tracy as Hemingway's Old Man and the Sea. There was a bridge keeper there also. His tiny green house was near the bridge, somewhat shielded by a mature fig tree. It was very quiet then and there; hardly anyone lived out here, the Cajun Coop was not built yet and there was no Emile Verret Road. Instead, there was an old wooden store sitting in the exact spot that currently begins this, now, much traveled road.

This memory was from a long time ago when the world was big and still and discreet. Something as simple as going to the old store for a grape corn sucker was eventful and sitting in a car at night with the windows rolled down in the middle of nowhere (without a cell phone) waiting for the bridge to close was safe. I would listen to the sounds coming from the bayou and perhaps hear a faraway freight train, never fearing anything in the dark stillness of the country, hearing only peaceful noises from the natural world as I sat snuggly in the backseat of our car and waited to cross over. Anyway, I sat there for a while and the soothing breeze, and the sound of the tugboat helped me to remember time, that time when my thoughts were original and not spiked with racket and endless propaganda and my world was safe.

September 2019

The world is very busy now. Information comes at us even when we try to hide, too much information, much of it useless and meant only to provoke, that's what I think. I threaten, at least once a week, to disconnect, to go back to how things were just a decade ago but then, I don't; I don't think we can anymore. It was Darwin that said, "It is not the strongest or the most intelligent who will survive but those who can best manage change." I might be doomed.

Aside from the noise we hear each day, there is still so much beauty to see from our starship. It is August now and the last days of summer are here. More memories have been made, memories like those I began this piece with memories that will comfort in winter when the sun is illusive and the coldness seeps through, memories that will still be there when new bridges are built. There is a sudden darkness now as the late summer sun sets and the moonlight takes command. Some nights I wait for the elusive falling star knowing, but wondering, how the moon will move to my kitchen window the next morning when I most certainly have left it hanging over the woods. It seems so distant and different outside of the kitchen window as the day takes from it its glory. And there is the sun beneath it, another day, no matter what is happening here, it sits and watches, doing what it must. It dries the dew on each blade of grass, it opens the blossoms on the late summer flowers and stimulates the honeybees. It is unlike the moon, it is powerful in a physical way, it is basic, and it is forceful. The moon lets you gaze at it and dream on it. It is not as (visibly) constant as the sun, sometimes it does not show up and the night sky is not as peaceful but then, it appears as a sliver amongst the stars on a clear night and I stop to admire it as my thoughts soften and all the world seems mystical and beautiful as the night blankets all that is wrong.

As I welcome the seventh month, I know the bloom of summer has peaked, but much is left to enjoy especially in the early morning. My bees are busiest then, preparing for their excursions to find what is left of the summer nectar, fanning the hive before the heat of the day makes a bit of coolness impossible and tidying up the supers where, hopefully, more honey can be extracted in early fall. Busy busy, as I try not to be.

September 2019

This is the weekend of sprayed on silver hair, cowboy boots from Gulotta's, red bandanas for the Farmer's Parade, an ocean of empty beer cans covering Main Street after the Fais do - do, friends and strangers in the park, sweaters and jean jackets, art in the Armory, fresh baked cakes and blue ribbons in the basement, cute lambs and well fed cows in the shed and being squashed on the Tilt a Whirl, at least that's how I remember it...Sugar Cane Festival weekend. It was fun, it was festive, and it was in the City Park.

Life was slower then, events seemed greater, and distractions seemed fewer. Halloween was "declared" in mid-October when Charlie Brown aired on CBS (no DVR to record it, you had to be there) and wax "lips" and "black mustaches" showed up at the grocery store candy counter. Thanksgiving was the fourth Thursday in November and your teacher "ran off" Pilgrims and cornucopias on the ditto machine to color and to decorate the classroom. And believe it or not, Christmas was in late December then. We decorated our Douglas Fir around December 15th with fat-colored lights, glass ornaments covered in last year's "snow" and tangled lots of tinsel. Main Street was decorated, store windows were adorned in Christmas magic, a little toy store opened in the back of J W Lowes across from Mr. Huckabee's lunch counter and the Sear's Wish Book had come in the mail, it was December, it was, finally, the Christmas season.

One holiday at a time, one season at a time; that's how it was. Today, I can watch Linus in the pumpkin patch anytime I want from my phone, I'm not sure where to find the minimally marketable Thanksgiving, the WishBook is no longer and the Christmas "season" begins in September, sitting on shelves right next to Halloween.

September 2019

I could be outside from daybreak to nightfall in these late September days. In the very early morning, if I squint and try hard, I can see the season slowly and subtly changing, going from the green and lush of late summer to the barely brown and crisp of early fall. The air is sometimes clear from dampness and there are faint noises of wild rabbits in the woods, sensations and rustles reminding me how wonderful and restoring Nature is. The Full Hunter Moon will rise on the 13th as the familiar smell of roux seeps through the air near Boulingy Plaza, Charlie Brown will be on TV to complete the arrival of autumn and Halloween will end this most loved month that will begin in just two days. I hope to be there absorbing the full and fleeting wonder of this entrance into this cozy season and not somewhere down the road rushing to the next big thing.

I end this piece with a quote from Linus, something shrewd, noteworthy, and perhaps humorous in these turbulent times of "overenthusiastic" opinions, "There are three things I've learned never to discuss with people: religion, politics, and the Great Pumpkin."

October 2019

"What will be left?", a deep-thinking question Adele and I pondered amid a light conversation about the pan she used to bake the day's cornbread. This brief and probing conversation was on a morning this week before our store opened. The ovens were on, the soups were steeping, and another day was beginning, just a seemingly ordinary day. But, for me, it was an extraordinary day; it was the day after I had visited a doctor about a health concern, something suspicious on my skin. It had been a scary few days prior, days of anxiety and morbid wonder, thus, the question Adele and I contemplated. The worry had clouded my days but then, thankfully, I was given good news from a good doctor, someone local and wonderful. Anyway, within those worrisome days, a veil was lifted, and I saw many things differently, more depth was revealed and more compassion towards others was found; another rich layer of life was added. I realized, once again, how unimportant much of what we value is; things that really matter can only be felt with the heart, as I remind myself, "what will be left",

And speaking of things that matter, at least for me, home has become my most favorite place to be, especially this time of year. I remember reading somewhere that Emily Dickinson never left home for 26 years. When I read this long ago, I thought that idea was strange and eccentric, but now, I find it slightly enviable.

Except for a trip to visit my children and now and then to a place far away, I think I could be happy just staying home each day. I have spent years unwittingly setting up "centers" for myself around here – a collection of fruit trees, paths that lead to nowhere in the woods, a sunny place to paint, a quiet spot to write, my hopeful and sometimes hopeless gardens, the chickens, my bees, the small burning pile near the woods, the keeping room at sundown when the light filters through the blinds and a fresh cup of coffee to sip while I watch it set, and my kitchen filled with smudges, spices and scents of home. Home is really my favorite place to be. I have learned, through much time and discipline, to (try to) overlook the boundless lists of "to dos" around here and concentrate on the loveliness of the "as is". Because of that shift in attitude, I feel more contentedness and less anxiety about the endless projects a home requires. I must put forth tremendous effort to maintain this stable state of mind, but I have become much better at it now. Home is a place to soothe, it is a place to retreat, a place where our lives happen; it is a place to gather yourself. I find delightful stories in the little piles of life throughout this house, they have become narratives for me instead of heaps of "clutter", small venues that tell the story of the people who live here…books that are read, projects that are underway, tales of everyday life, both long ago and now.

Anyway, all is well here with me for now as I vow to make more efforts to maintain my health and to be more aware of the circumstances of others, especially those going down the tough roads we all may travel, while realizing, once again, that family, friends, our home, and our health are the important components of life. And to the question, "What will be left?", I answer, it will be the feelings of love we shared and gave that will remain. "Love what matters."

November 2019

With the winter, comes the patchy darkness in my head….it sometimes seeps in through the sunshine of my life just as the cold air sometimes quietly creeps beneath the backdoor. I can't help it, it just does. I suppose it comes with this age, this time when you have lived for these many years and have been both a participate and a spectator of many events along the way. Some of the "events" have been wonderful, some have been somber…all have been effective and have gathered eternally on the shelves of my life. Most days, the shiny and bright occasions encapsulate my thoughts and enrich my days but sometimes the broken keepsakes of life come into focus, for whatever reason, and they direct me, today is that day.

Like you, I have many blessings, the grandest one being my family, but also, like you, there have been times where my world was broken. These impending days of winter seem to remind me. I write this because, alongside of winter, are the "Holidays" and as shiny and bright as they may be for some, they can cast shadows of barrenness for others. We should all be aware and supportive.

Thankfully, the sun has come out after the sudden and killing dip of winter and things are bright again...life ebbs and flows. The fronts are struggling to find their way into this delta and change is in the air for certain. The ground is mottled with intensely colored leaves and the woods are tinted with ambers and burgundies, all under an azure sky that darkens suddenly now instead of the slow dimming brilliance of the summer one-

Nature is busy preparing this glorious season and the new moon will rise, once again, on the 26th.

The woods will soon be draped with cobwebs that will extend over the paths – masterpieces in the early fall mornings with dew outlining their shapes and emphasizing their details – little Rembrandts of the night that will remind me of chalk artist in today's cities – working so hard to create, only to be dissolved by a certain looming force of nature, yet doing this work all over again the next day, knowing the inevitable result.

These days of autumn will roll out like a tapestry rug – each hour offering something different than the one before, like the chapters of our lives, unfolding and delivering little pieces of art that delight us and then disappear into the morning light of the next day where, if we look with open eyes, we will see yet another masterpiece beginning, a wonderful moment to add to the shelves of our lives.

I hope you can find those moments to look forward to within this holiday season that is (abruptly) upon us, whether it is a child coming home for the holidays, a trip you may take or, simply, a ripe orange in your backyard. Try not to lose them in the turmoil of the season for they will be there for you when you may need to dispel the patchy darkness of winter; they will give you the warmth you need.

I extend heartfelt good wishes to you for Thanksgiving and encouragement to be grateful for all you have and feel much happiness throughout these beautiful days of autumn. But most importantly, I extend inspiration that we can all be supportive of those who may feel empty during these times of family, friends, and festivities, that we can be the light in someone's darkness.

December 2019

I love being outside in winter. I want to see all that nature reveals when she sheds her colorful coat of autumn. What culinary treats lie beneath the mighty oaks, where do the dragonflies of summer go when the last month begins and how big has the bunny family that lives in the woods grown to be?

I want to watch the fronts roll in from the North and the West and then see the tiny northern visitors lined up on the wires as I drive home and watch the hungry hawks floating over the cane fields hunting for dinner. I want to see the frost on my neighbor's roof early in the morning before the sun quickly melts it and watch the squirrels scurrying for the last bit of acorns beneath the Live Oaks. I want to gather gifts from the December yard — citrus from the trees, camellias to put in vases that were a birthday present from a dear friend and pinecones that have fallen from the trees near the road. I love the reveal; I love the nakedness of winter and the wonder of December.

Inside, within the bareness and the stolen quietness, within this house that will soon be filled with family and sound, I try to recall the details of past Decembers. I think of the subtle warmth and the people there to make it special, their voices and laughter and the heartfelt biddings of "Merry Christmas" but, thankfully, I struggle to remember what worries may have been dimming the magic. This lack of recollection makes me think about time and its magical effect, its purpose, really. I think of the figurative concept of "moving through time". It carries us forward, as it must and it washes away the troubles and concerns, leaving behind just the good stuff - like little pebbles on the beach after the tide rolls out - smooth and shiny and brilliant from a cleansing; that is what is left of the Decembers, a rich golden resin that was our past.

January 2020

I drug the Christmas tree to the burn pile one recent morning. It is a guilty pleasure I suppose to burn my very dead tree, but I compost nearly everything else so, I burn my tree. I will sit there on a winter afternoon in January, and I watch the fire while giving it a fond farewell. Along the way to its final resting place, icicles fell from its branches. They are there in the winter yard and I know that this spring, when I cut the grass these fragments of this Christmas' adornments will catch the light of the warm spring sun and glisten; I will see them and think of now. I will remember this Christmas. I leave them where they are, and I say adieu to this holiday season and a warm good-bye to the tree that occupied a special place our home for a while.

I have not been outside in a few days, so I explored a bit to see what winter had done. It has brought visitors from the North - small warblers camouflaged in the winter grass that seem to make the ground move as they do; it was enchanting to see them once again. And the starkness of the woods helped me to see through and be thankful for the lushness of summer but enjoying this moment to "look within". The rabbits are there hiding in their holes and now and then darting about looking for food, sometimes I see their backsides - their cottontails - bounding about and I naturally think of Peter! And the raccoons come out at night, looking for food and threatening the smaller animals, I know that because of my vulnerable chicken population (sometimes I forget to close the door to the coop). Winter is challenging for animals and people.

I did find more camellias near the woods. I thought they were over by now but there are some left – almost a revitalization. Anyway, I picked a few for inside and one smaller one especially to sit in a Christmas present, a tiny pot Elizabeth made for me in her high school pottery class, one of my most treasured Christmas gifts. Even in winter there is beauty to bring inside.

I suppose that is what I'm trying to say with this assemblage of words, trying to remind you and me how each season has its purpose and its beauty – just as each season of our lives has its. Like spring and summer, our beauty and purpose are very much apparent in our youth but as we continue, like winter, the landscape becomes a bit more puzzling, and our path must be "repurposed". As an art student I painted old, weathered faces – had a fascination with and regard for the miles of life that were evident – years and years of wisdom, wisdom that needed a place to be. They found a place on my canvases that now hang on my walls and in my thoughts that, now, remind me of their beauty.

We all have "places to be" always, in each season of our lives. Just like the woods in winter, as time goes on, time gives us more opportunity to look within and redefine.

Read the poem beneath and the first time you read it, think of it literally, think of the seasons, and them read it again and think of it figuratively and substitute the seasons of nature for the seasons of your life...

"There is a privacy about it which no other season gives you…. In spring, summer and fall people sort of have an open season on each other; only in the winter, in the country, can you have longer, quiet stretches when you can savor belonging to yourself". Ruth Stout

Enjoy each season... of your life.

February 2020

I took a walk through my very soggy yard one morning after the relentless rain and wondered, where was winter? I do not particularly care about being cold, but I believe we need the Old Man. He helps to control the mosquito population and gives our plants a rest before the hurry and flurry of spring and, equally important, he keeps me inside to catch up on things in my house before the warmer weather insist that I spend all my time in the yard. Anyway, I could not find him. Instead, there were tiny birds chatting on the telephone wire near the road, a sweet familiar fragrance in the air and a peculiar little wind that floated through the neighborhood. Could that be spring? Are those little birds our northern visitors or are they our little birds returning from Mexico and the woods? I wish I knew.

For some reason, the curious wind kindled some stirring thoughts in my head, thoughts about the words we speak and their influence on the memories we keep. Like some of you, perhaps most of you reading this, I have people in my life that are not here anymore. I carry their memory with me and continue to love them as many of the moments of my day remind me. I hear their voices that repeat the things they have said to me, words that make them immortal. These people that I remember and their voices I hear are not only close family members but, sometimes, casual friends or people I have met only once and would never see again but their words stayed with me.

This hint of spring that I write of causes a remembrance of a distant neighbor, Mrs. Viator, someone with the most delightful and uninhibited garden of flowers and food. One afternoon long ago, while walking through her patch of paradise, she told me that her garden is why, on some days, she is anxious to wake up, anxious to see what has grown or changed from the day before. I understand that and think of her words many times throughout the seasons. Her words encourage me to plant more now so that, later, when I am older, I have more to be amazed by, more to wake up to and enjoy.

Each day and nearly every moment within, I think of my much-loved sister, Susan, whose whimsical words often dance around in my worried head and help to calm me. Her words that were once spoken in casual conversations, are now cherished, and continually humming in my head. Many times, in times of stress and doubt, I think of her and her words of comfort she has said to me; words that still soothe me and keep her near.

And the silly sayings from my dad that I often took for granted pop up when needed and not expected to remind me of his laughter and how much I miss it. Just yesterday, Andrew quoted him in a conversation with Matthew, "How about them apples?", affectionately articulated from, seemingly, nowhere. I was happy to know that their grandpa, my dad, was still "there" and still so reachable.

And, of course, my mother is always "talking" to me. There are so many words, so many moments to remember her by. She is almost always the voice in my head. These ethereal thoughts I write of are remembered because of words spoken, words that have become what remains of love and time.

Anyway, the little wind is still now but has left behind these contemplations, thoughts that make me realize how important our words are.

The words of great thinkers and legendary people are written in books and inscribed on monuments but the words of the people we love are etched on our hearts. We should take care with what we say, for it is our words, that will remain. How about them apples?

March 2020

It was "that" night, that summer night I think about when it is not summer. The moon rose and it was full, a Full Buck Moon, the time when tiny antlers emerge from the new bucks, and the locust were uttering under the one street light near my house and the chimney swifts were diving for mosquitos while the tree frogs sang their glorious song – it was there, all of summer condensed into one perfect night – I had a front row seat to all of this unexpected bliss. I am not sure why this bucolic thought came to mind, perhaps it was the Full Worm Moon and the hint of spring dangling throughout the woods and evident in the busy hives, I'm not sure, but it seemed redeemable, it seemed like a nice thought amongst the not so nice climate of corona fear and political fear and all that is wrong with the world fear. Nature is my go-to drug and while it is ever changing, it never disappoints, especially now, now that I am older and have more time and interest in its occurrences.

The natural beauty from our starship, that's where my thoughts linger – about the Full Buck Moon in a clear July sky I recall. This is about these summer days that will keep warm thoughts in your winter head as you remember the cicadas that had made their ascent from the dark earth only to mate and then to die and the sounds of the night as much busyness takes place amongst the nocturnal animals, animals that have been pushed from their habitats as cities and towns sprawl but I still hear many of them here. I sometime catch the racket of the raccoons following the bayous looking for food and mischief and while I fear for my hens, I love the reassurance that they still have space to run and the reassurance that the hot summer sun will drive out the germs that are making many sick….Mother Nature to the rescue, Mother Nature to help the hands that heal.

Again, sudden darkness where the sun sets, and the moonlight takes command as I wish I knew more about constellations. I wait for the elusive falling star and always wonder exactly how the moon moved to my kitchen window the next morning when I left it hanging over the woods. It seems so distant and different outside of the kitchen window as the day takes from it its glory. And there is the sun beneath it, another day, no matter what is happening here, there it sits doing what it must. It dries the dew on each blade of grass, it opens the blossoms on the summer flowers and stimulates the honeybees. It is unlike the moon, it is powerful in a physical way, it is basic, and it is forceful. The moon lets you gaze at it and dream on it. It is not as (visibly) constant as the sun, sometimes it doesn't show up and the night sky is not as peaceful but then, it appears as a sliver amongst the stars on a clear night and I stop to admire it as my thoughts soften and all the world seems mystical and beautiful as the night blankets all that is wrong.

Ironically, I write this ode to the moon, to the night, in daytime. The day is brilliant here with light and color and although the bloom of summer has not yet arrived, this early spring brings promise and sweet fragrances from the plum trees and tiny yellow flowers that cove the fields, much is there to enjoy especially in the early morning. My bees are busiest then, preparing for their excursions to find what is left of the summer nectar, fanning the hive before the heat of the day makes a bit of coolness impossible and tidying up the supers where, hopefully, more honey can be extracted in early fall. Busy busy, as I try not to be.

April 2020

I hang on to the small rituals of the day, I hang on because they are the things I can be certain of. I am happy to be in this somewhat bucolic space, this is the place I am used to, the place I know so well.

I know that the mockingbirds live in the white oak near the garden shed and that I will watch helplessly as they raid my biggest fig tree on July mornings. I know that there is a green lizard that lives behind the wooden shutter of my kitchen window and he will come out into the sun while I am making coffee each morning in spring as if to say hello and the tree frogs will sing with the moon rising and my honey bees will collect at the opening of the hive to feverishly fan keeping things bearable inside for the queen bee and her brood when the summer sun is nearly impossible. I know that I will pick magnolias throughout the spring and early summer and that the inevitable midsummer heat will soon be here for my zinnias and lantana, as the locusts arrive and circle streetlights while reminding me of childhood, just as the fireflies twinkling through the woods will do. I know I will pick honeysuckle vines for my kitchen and hang my laundry on days when there is no rain. I know the tides will roll in across the white sandy beaches along the Gulf Coast while I will be here, in the summer garden, picking cucumbers and eating fresh tomatoes in June. I know that home is a wonderful place to be and making any house a home only takes love and acts of kindness towards the ones who live there. I also know that good things and strength come from challenging times and that we will all find our way, it may not be as planned but it will still be good. These are some of the wonderful things I know.

I do not know what will happen next with this threatening virus. That is the uncertainty, that is where fear can, unfortunately, emerge and control.

My thoughts continue to drift, and I work persistently to stay in a place of positivity, a place of new growth and resurrection, a place called spring. I cannot think of a better way to end this column than with the wisdom of Pooh..." ...I've wandered much further today than I should, and I can't seem to find my way back to the Wood. So, help me if you can I've got to get back to the House at Pooh Corner by one. You'd be surprised there's so much to be done, count all the bees in the hive, chase all the clouds from the sky..."

I hope you find your way within these days of insecurity and make good use of this time at home, for the rush of the world is waiting right outside of your door. I wish you a Happy Easter and a blessed Passover.

May 2020

The houses were smaller then and in the late afternoon when kitchen windows were open the neighborhood smelled like supper. Walter Cronkite's familiar voice would be part of the background concerto along with the banging screen door and the occasional quick piercing ring of the telephone. The carport held only a single spot for the family car, fireflies were caught and called lightning bugs, and the dining room table was where supper and homework happened. The windows had curtains on them, either homemade or ordered from Sears and Roebuck's and there was only one TV; it was in the living room, and it signed off at midnight.

I am not just describing my house, I am describing everyone's house in my childhood. I am just taking my senses back a few decades to that "simple life"; noting, we are suddenly "simply" there again, in different ways.

A few years ago, Elizabeth and I took a trip to New England. It was one of the best trips of my life. I especially remember and was impacted by Concord, Massachusetts and wrote about it when I returned...

"Most of today was spent in Concord, MA amongst the transcendentalists – Emerson, Thoreau, and their little tag along, Louisa Mae. Just this morning, I stood in Louisa Mae Alcott's bedroom and saw the desk her father made for her where she wrote *Little Women* and just after that I was at The Manse and saw the garden that Henry David Thoreau planted for his friend Nathaniel Hawthorne and Sophia Hawthorne's 1843 window etching – "Man's accidents are God's purposes".

On that day, we also walked around Walden Pond and through the woods at Walden where Thoreau went to "live deliberately". These two quotes I felt compelled to cite 8 years ago, two thoughts I thought were interesting and profound, are now two thoughts that can fit seamlessly into the fabric of today.

As I reread them, I wonder what social disturbance was occurring then to produce such reflection from Sophia Hawthorne and Thoreau. Anyway, just a fragment of a thought, a casual observation and a beautiful memory joined together and sitting here on this page to perhaps ponder and to recognize life's repetition.

As with all things, good and not so good behaviors have come from this present-day "disturbance". Something "good" is the seemingly increased interest in gardening. Going to the garden early in the morning to see what the night has brought is a simple and pure joy I wish for all. Mother Nature will have done her magic in the hours before under the moonlight, below the stars and within the shadowy shroud of nightfall. Her morning gifts will be polished with dew and filled with flavor and goodness. The birds will be there at dawn also, morning birds, already chirping and speaking to one another through song drifting in the cerulean sky and perched slightly hidden in the trees.

I always listen and try to understand knowing, that no matter what, Nature will continue to do what she does; the birds will always sing, the flowers will reseed and bloom again and again, and the night will deliver the dew.

I love that she has so much power and determination. I love that she can sustain us and to give us nourishment and joy and I especially love how we have, in this slow down, come to know her once again. She is like our mothers in many ways, always there, always giving, always teaching.

Happy Mother's Day to all the moms, to the ones still with us and to the mothers, sisters, aunts, grandmothers, girlfriends, and wives who remain with us in spirit and whose essence is continued through our love and our lives. And to all of you, happy gardening...

Take good care of your mother and take good care of our Earth, for "A good mother is irreplaceable" Adriana Trigian

June 2020

Our thirteen-year-old dog passed away. She was the last "family" dog, one of the pups in a litter of mutts. It was Elizabeth's turn to have a dog, so, she made the choice and picked a cute little black puppy with a white face and a "waggly tail" and named her Baja, a curious and strange name.

I do not know where the unusual name came from and I am not sure she does either but, at twelve years old, that was the name she chose. Through the years, Baja grew comfortably into the odd name; she grew up to be odd, quirky, loved, and now, missed, very much missed.

She was always there in my peripheral vision. She watched me in the mornings as I fed my chickens, she sat at the door and waited for me to come home, and she barked when a stranger came. She contributed much to our family and all she wanted in return was food, water, and someone to rub her stomach and call her name.

I walked through the woods this morning, her domain, a place she commanded, to think of her, to feel her presence somehow. I remembered how she sometimes chased wild rabbits and sat relentlessly with her nose down a rabbit hole until some action occurred, tail wagging and chops licking, determined and patient. She was ailing these last few weeks but through it all, through her discomfort, when the sun painted a patch of glorious rays on the grass in the middle of the afternoon, she found it and laid on her back, four legs in the air soaking it in. I would watch her from my kitchen window as she lay there in complete rhythm with the world helping me to understand that moments are precious, too precious to waste and, maybe, we should capture life as it presents itself for, like the warm sunbeams, it is fleeting.

I also learned about forgiveness from Baja. I learned that even though she made me mad when she buried bones or bagels in my just made flower bed, and I fussed at her sternly she soon after would stand in front of me with big brown eyes that told me it was okay that I got mad at her and said those awful things; she still loved me and we would "move on". She held no grudges.

We learn a lot from our pets, children learn a lot. They learn about responsibility and compassion, and they come to realize how fragile life is and how ephemeral the moments are. And when they die, they learn about love and loss. I hope all of you have had a "Baja" in your life at some point, a pet to remind you of the innocence and purity that exists amongst the darkness that sometimes tries to dominate our world.

I am drenched in summer by now and I feel the world slowing down, getting gentler while the afternoons linger, and the nights are a spectacle with the waning Full Strawberry Moon dangling like an ornament in the nearly summer sky and the June bugs here with their sturdy shield reminding us of the sultry nights that will soon come to be. The green and blue dragonflies skim the water of the pool and settle on the wire of my clotheslines as we wait for the Gulf to, perhaps, deliver its wrath. In the meantime, amongst all that is unhealed and uncertain, we can still be kind to our neighbor, love our dog, plant a garden, take in the sunbeams, and remember, we all are what we learn.

July 2020

I fall asleep at night wishing for the sudden arrival of morning, a quiet and wonderful place I go to every day. Every day I say a silent pray of gratefulness that I am here walking the familiar few steps to my kitchen. Making coffee, raising the blinds, and saying a hushed hello to the little upside-down squirrel in the elm tree who is always busy stealing the bird feed. I then go to my small makeshift studio to see the sun, who has, through the night, taken the place of the moon, as it peeps through the undressed windows. It is a simple ritual, but so important. Coffee is on and TV is off as I try to harmonize with the new day.

These mornings are far away from the "brisk" mornings of my youth. Then, I was awakened suddenly by wind up alarm clocks, a baby's hungry cry, or a child's energetic flight down the stairs ...abrupt wake up sounds that once filled this house with much energy, movement and love. Now, it's a morning bird at my bedroom window that wakes me up.

It is summer and somewhat quieter outside my bedroom window, however. The hurry and hum of the spring is over. The baby birds are grown; they have left the nest and their mothers have less to do these days. I am thinking they are flying with more liberation and less hurry as they rest from the hasty spring mornings of hungry baby birds and dangerous skies. I hear them again in the late afternoon, their sounds are not as soothing as the morning sounds, they are, instead, nearly deafening as they compete with the tree frogs and locusts.

The Full Buck Moon is in the night sky as it changes from June to July. Nocturnal bugs collect around our porch lights at dusk and the cicadas call in the middle of the day when the heat is deep, and the trees are still. Our gardens have been hit by the heat, but the okra continues to grow tall and stately as though it were in the West African sun, giving us food for our summer table and winter gumbos. Celeste Figs are simmering on stoves and canning jars are popping as this month of heat and fireworks travels swiftly by. Soon, the bees will share their honey with us, and the earth will be prepared for yet another bounty of fall vegetables to grow in our backyards or purchase at our farmer's markets.

Nature will repeat her eternal march as we try, once again, to synchronize and stay in step with her faltering lead.

I end this rambling of words and images of the season with a humble thought and underlying wish for health and harmony in our small neighborhood of this big world. And, with the granting of this wish, I wish again that we extend our harmony to the next "neighborhood" and, as nature does, we all continue our march to the light.

August 27, 2020

Nineteen hundred ninety – two, that's where my memories travel as I sit here in silence twenty-eight years later. The wrath of Hurricane Andrew had just hit our town and tore us up. Much of our heritage was taken by the whirling winds of this insistent storm named Andrew. Our trees and houses were gone, our lives were uprooted alongside the massive oaks and brittle pines, how would this ever be us again? How do we begin to start over?

We did; we endured and worked and recovered. I wish that same sequel for our neighbors that were in the brutal path of Laura; I have seen the pictures.

On a simpler note, we did not have much technology to lose when Andrew hit. We lived in the country and were still using an antenna. There were no cellular telephones and no home computers but there was, nonetheless, a void, a modern vacuum had been formed by downed wires and fragmented cables; we were disconnected. Today, the day after Laura, I have little yard debris to pick up and my house is tight and secure but somehow, I feel more severed. This forfeit forces me to think how dependent I, we, have become on cable tv and internet and all things virtual. It makes clear how far removed many have become from all things real. I walk through the yard and see that my hens are still laying today, the bees are a little less busy but busy nevertheless, the two kittens from the woods are still shy and hungry, the mockingbirds are squawking, and the world still turning, the world that is always here and always genuine, the world that does not stop when unplugged.

in 1992, we felt somewhat abandoned by the modern world but not as much detachment as we feel in 2020. My boys still played outside then, and they only had Saturday morning cartoons to watch and VCR movies to rent, so that part of the aftermath was easy. I suppose it was just the oppressive heat that was the most bothersome. I do remember one beautiful occurrence that happened at night following that storm. The stars were unveiled. It was in a time before the use of generators was as widespread, so the night was somewhat quiet and the stars were blazing in the sky, it was before the matchless competition from down below. I will never forget that beauty, that real view of the night sky that, oddly, seemed unreal. I have not seen it again since.

I suppose we just thought things were upside down and weird with Covid, now we have the aftermath of a hurricane, now, we seem to be stretched to our outer bounds, now we are nowhere near our normal. Children are away from their schools, families are away from one another, stores and services are closed, and suspended and, within this odd setting, there are critical communal sounds that we all must decipher and deal with, together.

What else can be unveiled in this world of illusion, this world of skepticism where we search for the truth but many of our sources have been somewhat tainted as we hear extreme verses of the same song? For now, at least where I am on this day, I am without technology, without sounds from simulated sources and while I expect tomorrow to bring with it clean up and stifling heat, today, I meet face to face with my real world and question nearly everything.

September 2020

I don't really go many places these days, even in the days before Covid, I mostly stayed near home; tending my chickens, keeping my bees, planning my garden, and stressing over all that doesn't get done. I think I might be a pseudo hermit. But, sometimes, I am out, and I see some of you. And many of you comment on something I have written here. I notice that most all the comments you make are connected to something in nature. This, of course, makes me happy, because nature is somewhat of a lifeline for me and I love hearing that it is important to you also...a full moon in October and the leaves of Autumn, the ocean tides of summer and the cozy nip of winter followed by baby dragonflies and the freshness of spring, what could be better? Nature is a wonderful place to "go", it is where we can settle ourselves and find meaning.

I read Thoreau's Walden Pond in college (usually while sitting alongside of the lakes behind Miller dorm). In my craziest dreams, I never imagined, then, that I would see Walden Pond and the woods where Thoreau "wished to live deliberately", but I did. In 2012, Elizabeth and I sat beside its waters and walked the paths through the nearby woods. It was surreal, like stepping into a dream. Those moments have stayed with me as have the ordinary moments I have spent planting nearly, or possibly, a hundred trees and turning over warm spring soil each year for most of my life. Through all of this, my love has amplified, and my solace has grown deeper as I wish to "live deliberately".

Anyway, I am always happy that my mention of the natural world comforts another. In this world of "google everything" and FB fiction, nature remains steadfast and true to all of us. The downside to this 60 something year love affair I have is watching her disappear, watching her be used inconsiderately. I know we all need a place to live, and our population is growing, I understand that math, but I somehow think we can be kinder to her as we "progress". Maybe we can leave hints of her behind as we clear her meadows and maybe we can keep within our vision pieces of rainbows and glimmers of stardust, maybe we can consider her beauty, her future, and her purpose too.

The season is about to change; autumn has rolled in and there is much to absorb, much to do to greet it. I see hints of change in the woods, the green lush of late summer is subtly turning to the crisp brown of early fall and if you wake up early enough, the air is sometimes clear from dampness and the sounds are lucid, sounds of leaves and wild rabbits in the woods. The Harvest Moon will rise on October 1 this year; it is the full moon closest to the Autumnal Equinox, which was on September 22. Sounds and scents from inside are changing too, there are the welcome clatters of soup pots on the stove and subtle scents of spices from the oven, echoes and whiffs that remind me of years past, of times I thought would never end. These are the days of early fall when the woods turn colors, and the inner spaces are revealed.

It is time to, once again, turn over the soil and plant root crops and cruciferous vegetables for the Thanksgiving table and gather kindling for the winter fires. It's time to pull in and reflect and, hopefully, soon be with our families and friends. It is time to appreciate the bounty which is fall. I send out a subtle salute to our farmers and wish them all a successful and safe harvest. I have lived here for most of my life and each year in some way small or otherwise, I have acknowledged the Sugar Cane Festival; this year I do it with only words.

October 2020

The seasons are transitioning, slowly and unpredictably, from late summer to early autumn. Erik, our "soon to be" son in law, is nearly finished putting in our winter garden. Being from Massachusetts, he is new at this and is absorbing each twist and turn through the Louisiana random weather and unfamiliar environment with wonderment and pure joy. He is learning about the erratic seasons here and how winter turns to summer and suddenly back again and how we seamlessly take out our gumbo pots when the cool snap makes it down past I10 and put them away again when the warm breezes roll in from the Gulf; that's how it works "down here".

We will, hopefully and ultimately, have a bounty of cruciferous vegetables for soups and savor and a bounty of root crops for safe winter keeping in the pantry and in pickle jars. And when winter is over, we hope to harvest onions and garlic.

"When winter is over" …. how probing is this statement? What will be when winter is over? Who will we become by then? Will the virus continue to prevail, who will be our president, will some still be at odds with one another? It all seems so unknown like a cloud of uncertainty that hangs there close enough to touch but somewhat fearful to enter. Time will tell…

To end on a positive note, Halloween is on the night the Full Hunter's Moon rises, a Blue Moon. I wish for a minute I were a kid trick or treating and searching for the magic that this night will create, looking in shadows and searching for sounds that may be mystical. I love the small things this world gives us, the gifts from nature like the full moon and the distant howls and hoots of wild animals and I love the gifts the earth provides with a bit of toil and trouble from planting and nourishing. I love the display of subtle kindness shown for one another and our unyielding desire to help each other. I love the closeness of our community and the importance of our families, and I love reading and hearing things projected in love instead of hostility.

I hope you have a spooky Halloween and I hope you and I find a way to embrace all that we have and work to make what is lacking attainable.

I close with a tribute to yet another lost childhood tradition, the airing of the Peanuts series. Like all of you, I abound with fifty plus years of memories. I was a child when it first played on national TV in 1964. My imagination soared as I sat on our gold Naugahyde sofa with my little sister, Susan, as we became "friends" with Charlie Brown and his entourage. Then, when I had children of my own my mom or dad would always call with a reminder that Charlie and his crew would be on at 7 o'clock. Homework or whatever we were doing was put aside and we sat and watched, for how could it be Halloween without them? I am sad and I wish they could stay. Anyway, thanks for the memories, thanks for inserting purity into my childhood and that of my children and thank you for tapping into my imagination. Lastly, thank you Charlie Brown for this timely advice from your good buddy Linus, "I've learned there are 3 things never to discuss with people: religion, politics, and the Great Pumpkin". Goodbye Charlie Brown.

November 2020

The fronts are struggling to find their way into this delta but change, nevertheless, is in the air. The ground is mottled with intensely colored leaves and the woods are tinted with ambers and burgundies, all under an azure sky that darkens suddenly now instead of the slow dimming brilliance of the summer one - Nature is busy preparing this glorious season.

The cool and clear winds that blow now and then tell me Thanksgiving will soon be here. Oddly, these winds stir memories of my mother. After twenty-three years, I do not cry so much when I think of her, but I long, still. I long for a seat at her Thanksgiving table and family there, all of us. I long for that place where my dad would, "reliably", struggle with the Tom Turkey and my mom would wear an apron my grandmother had made for her years earlier, a checkered one with cross stitch embroidery threads and an ample sash that tied in a bow around her waist, moving around in the warmth of her kitchen with small children nearby and pots of autumn sweetness on the stove. I long for that endurance she seemed to have an infinite amount of, always there, always giving me, giving us, a safe place to rest, the giver, the miracle worker, the one who created the magic; she defined it for me and "big" days, like Thanksgiving, make the memory clearer. My heart softens as I think of those times of simple happiness especially up against the seeming strife of our modern world. Simple happiness, that is what I think of when I think of her and my life then, that is where I would like to steer towards with whatever remains of my journey.

I make a conscious effort to do this, finding joy and reason to celebrate underneath all the noise the world is causing right now, and this season is a promising time to pursue this illusive but worthwhile path. There are family recipes to share, dappled leaves falling in the cool wind to watch, firewood to cut and stack for the winter fires, cruciferous vegetables to grow or purchase at the market, strawberries to plant, and a full moon to sit beneath on the 30th. It will be the Full Beaver Moon. The name gives away its meaning…long long ago, when the November moon was its brightest, its light made easier work of setting traps for beavers that roamed the woods near the waterways; their fur was needed for the cold winter that was just ahead.

With these humble thoughts to ponder, I leave you with a wish for a Thanksgiving filled with ways to find happiness in its simplest and most pure form…perhaps a walk amongst the amber leaves, sharing your grandmother's handwritten recipe, ironing and using the heirloom tablecloth, watching the enigmatic sunset aflame with color, taking in the sweet and familiar smell of sugar from the mill and, most importantly, stepping away from the outside noise and putting yourself in a warm kitchen filled with scents of cinnamon, nutmeg and sounds of love. I hope we all can find simple happiness this Thanksgiving and the winter days that follow.

December 2020

I made a minestrone the day after our return from William and Lorena's beautiful San Antonio wedding. It is funny how we tend to go towards the little ordinary things in life after the big events. I suppose they are the familiar things, the quiet moments filled with everyday simple tasks, that bring us back to center. Today is one of those quiet days.

My Christmas tree is not decorated yet; it is sitting in a bucket of water with a fresh cut soaking up the moisture. Soon, it will be filled with lights and glass bulbs, soon, it will be Christmas 2020. I try to remember Christmas past, especially the Christmases my mom told me about her childhood during the Great Depression when times were (very) hard for everyone. I remember the mention of fresh fruit that was sometimes in her stocking, citrus mostly. That was her only gift. I never pick an orange from my tree without thinking of that, without thinking of how easily I do this and how scarce it was for a little girl in the 1930s. I think about how the Depression finally ended only to be followed by the War and how within that time, her father succumbed to a heart attack and her mother was left with 5 children to care for. I do remember her stories. She told them to me, not to dishearten me, but to perhaps, put them in my mind to use as a measuring tool when times would be bad for me or for our world. Maybe this Christmas is one of those times, maybe it is a time to reflect more than usual, maybe we should feel encouraged by what happened before in our country and how our parents, grandparents and great grandparents survived it and continued to grow and contribute.

Anyway, I will decorate my tree and wrap presents and be grateful for all that I have as I think of my mother and those before us who endured but ultimately overcame and were strong.

Some of my last words for Berry Tales 2020 are of a selfish nature; they are words about my son, William. He and Lorena's wedding was lovely and for the most part, I "held up" well, even during their magical and poignant vows. But then, William surprised me with a mother son dance to my all-time favorite song, "He Walked on Water" by Randy Travis and every bit of "proud mama" emotion burst from my heart and I cried. I will forever remember the enchantment of William and Lorena's wedding, the union of two becoming one before friends, family and

God under a Texas sky that went from a brilliant blue to a dusky backdrop of twinkling stars as our hearts were filled with love.

I close with a Happy Hanukah and a Merry Christmas to all of you and wishes for a wonderful New Year, I mean that sincerely. Skip and the kids (that happen to be here) will light the first candle of Hanukah this evening and I will soon string lights on the tree, simple tasks that will bring us joy.

As I wait to watch the Christmas sky turn to twinkles and wonderment, I hope that this very unusual holiday season reveals something out of the ordinary that becomes a moment we will hold on to, a moment like my special dance with my son. Today, on this December day, my heart is full, and I am home, remembering, and happy in my familiar kitchen making minestrone.

January 2021

I begin this new year's column with a quote that seemed to randomly appear within my orb, and I thought you might find prophetic and perhaps, amusing to ponder. It is by Zora Neale Hurston, a folklorist and writer, among other things. She writes, "There are years that ask questions and years that answer."

I think 2020 was one of the years that asked us the most questions ever. Hopefully, we will find some suitable answers in 2021.

My friend Lucy Hunnicutt also wrote something I would like to share, something that has given me a "soft place to land" amongst the turmoil that is now. She wrote, "Joy in January might come about with a bird feeder. A simple bird feeder right outside your window. If possible, hang a bird feeder outside a window near where you work or sit...or eat. This will increase your joy and happiness by a factor of 10...Let's just say ten but really, I think it's more. Do it. "It is something so simple that gives so much.

One thing I do know and have always known, Nature still holds everything. It holds life and joy and peace, sustenance, and answers. It is there for all of us no matter where we are. For some, the natural world is abundant and sprawling, it is forests and meadows and streams and oceans. For others, it is a clay pot of soil on a balcony and a red geranium in spring or a bird on a wire in a city scape or a small dandelion forcing its way into life through cracks in the cement, or an ordinary backyard transformed into a beguiling vegetable garden with daisies and zinnias planted amongst the rows, either way, it is there. I have spent so much time in my life worrying about our natural world, so much time fearing its demise. I, like all others, have done harm, for to live in comfort, it seems we must use resources. But, as time goes and our footprint becomes more evident, I feel more and more inclined to do better, to use less. Perhaps these simple words I write on this hometown paper will inspire someone and then someone will inspire another and another and more thought will be given to nature and all she does for us. Maybe we can all do a better job taking good care of her and enjoying all that she is.

I make these references just in time for our state's Arbor Day, the third Friday in January. We have lost so many trees this year from hurricanes, perhaps it would be a good idea to plant a few more. And when your tree grows bigger and you grow older, perhaps you can hang a bird feeder on it and, later, when you are home more, perhaps you can watch with delight the birds you feed and as my friend Lucy says, "increase your joy and happiness by a factor of 10."

The moon will be full on the 28th this month. It is the Full Wolf Moon. Long ago in the dead of winter, packs of hungry wolves roamed and howled searching for food in the cold and barren landscape and the full January moon helped in their search. I suppose that still occurs today in remote forest and woods. The thought in my head seems magical, the actual sight would be terrifying, however.

Welcome 2021. Let the questions of 2020 be answered and with them, some form of peace and comfort be restored to all. Plant a tree, feed the winter birds, find joy; it still exists.

February 2021

This will be a love letter, a "valentine", to all of you and to this town…

For a bit over a year now, I have been looking at New Iberia, and all Acadiana, through the eyes of my daughter, Elizabeth, and her fiancé, Erik. Elizabeth seems to have had some sort of awakening regarding her hometown, she sees it seemingly for the first time; the ordinary has become special.

And Erik really is seeing it for the first time and never wants to leave. He is enchanted with the landscape and the people. He has found much joy in the land and beneath the sun, spending endless summer hours happily working in the garden in the hot southern sun, loving all things Louisiana.

Because of them, it is as though I too have rediscovered this town, this town of which I am not a native but found myself here in November of 1960, in Miss June Boudreaux's first grade class at Susan Terrell. Mr. Burt Terrell was the principal and I sat across the aisle from Ronald Brumley in the back of the classroom, the new girl's desk. We read from Dick and Jane readers each day and had number aides, ditto color sheets of Pilgrims, and ice cream recess.

The town was "new" then, it was fascinating. So much was going on here. There were neighborhood grocery stores like Dugas' and Dartez's and big stores like A & P and Winn Dixie. There were barber shops and beauty shops and dime stores and doctors who made house calls and school yards filled with little girls in dresses hand sewn with rik rak and covered buttons and little boys hanging upside down from monkey bars. There was a park with friendly squirrels and roller skating and little shops to buy fresh oysters and bowling alleys with Friday night leagues and filled up churches scattered throughout. There were PTA meetings in the evenings with parents filling the school auditorium and the principal dressed in a suit and all the teachers there to help while moms and dads visited tidy classrooms filled with kid's work and tiny desks in neat rows. There were privately owned drugstores like Ackal's and shoe stores with Bannock Devices to measure little feet. There was a movie theater where it was safe to be for a Saturday afternoon. Mothers could take clothes on approval from Abdalla's, ladies could find white gloves and bolts of fabric at Wormser's and Easter hats waited in the windows at Bowab's and Creim'Many have left, many have moved down the road and far away, but those who have returned, I believe, are happy that they did, just as Terry Pratchett so fitting says, "Why do you go away? So that you can come back. So that you can see the place you came from with new eyes and extra colors. And the people there see you differently, too..."

As I close this "Valentine", I must also say "thank you" to the very source that this article appears on, the Daily Iberian. They have reached out to Elizabeth several times and generously written about her and Erik's future café. Small towns are the best towns, and this is that town.

Thank you, New Iberia, and all your wonderful people that we have had the honor of meeting and the joy of living amongst. I see it all, once again, through the eyes of my children and it is especially lovely this time around. Let us be that community, that community that supports one another and speaks through love and seeks to improve what we have. As the world struggles to find peace, let us be that wonderful place called home.

March 2021

There is an asparagus fern in my garden that I treasure. The freeze nipped it...I will wait and hope. It is an irreplaceable plant; it was the last birthday present from my sister, Susan. She repotted it from one of our mother's plants, one she had taken from the yard when we sold our parent's house; we divided it and brought it to our houses; it was something alive that we could take care of. I had lost mine one winter long ago so, for my birthday, she shared hers with me. I remember that summer day, in June nearly four years ago, I remember her driving up with the fern, unexpectedly. It was potted in a purple pot and fresh green from the spring and early summer sun. I was so happy. It was as though we were sharing our mother for a moment, it was something only a sister would know how to do, would know how much it meant, this living thing, this gift of nature repotted once again and shared once again...energy from the earth extending the memory of our mother. Anyway, the blast of cold may have ended that extension...time will tell.

Within the unexpected package of Artic cold we lit fires in the masonry fireplace and stayed warm under blankets and inside of sweaters. I dug around the corners of my house, inside forgotten cabinets, deep in the bottom of drawers and underneath familiar belongings. I found many "missing" things but my most intriguing discovery were my journals, journals from a life far away from here, a life in the 70s where youth was defined by discovery and the world was waiting to be explored, where all things were possible. There was very little "noise" when these journals were written; I had my own thoughts, my own direction and interpretation of the world. The handwritten words from long ago prompted me to remember how big I thought the earth was, how large the span of forests and wilderness and how mysterious faraway lands and their people were. And how cities were places of extreme energy and opportunity. I wrote about boyfriends and school and going places and I wrote about the nearby ...the sunsets, the flora, and my pets. It seemed so simple. I think what struck me most was the lack of influence in my writings, these thoughts were mine, they were developing without the soil of the world, without external influence. Moments in time written down...I fear that may be lost soon, the written word, the solitude of our thoughts expressed without rumor.

I wait for the healing sun to do its magic in my yard. I hope my asparagus fern still has life, for it has been my lifeline of sorts for many years, my jolt that reminds me of my mother and my sister each time I walk by it and as always, I hope for slower moments, moments that give me time to absorb all that is around me, moments that allow me time to reach out to people, those people that I sometimes miss, moments to dig underneath things, in the bottom of drawers and behind little doors discovering a place of safety and secrecy .

I have a cute thought to sum up with a small incidental goal I have in the remainder of my life...it is something I remember from my youth. Miss Sue, someone I have written about and someone I have carried in my heart for nearly my entire life did so many wonderful things with her days. One thing she did was cook rice for her cats, cats that came from the woods and sat on her steps and meowed. Now, at 66, I too would like to have those slow moments in time, slow enough and pure enough to cook rice for a cat.

April 2021

The beekeepers came this week. I watched as the sedative smoke surrounded the hives and the faint smell of honey reached across the field. I never get tired of that sight, nature at its purest, life at its foundation.

It is Spring now and the early mornings are an invitation I cannot decline. There are bird songs all through the woods and the waning Worm Moon hangs behind my Sycamore tree silently observing before the world wakes up, the human world, for the world of nature has been awake for hours. I cannot help but feel joy when I hear their songs and gratitude that I can. I go outside many mornings of the week just to push away some of the heaviness of life and replace it with joy. Sorrow sometimes returns, but it is a broader sort, it returns because I think of the many people, especially children, who are not able to hear the sounds of birds or see the first blooms of spring and baby dragonflies and tiny white and lavender flowers in meadows and fields. Those simple sights and sounds were a large part of our distant childhoods, clover flower necklaces, spring days filled to the brim with nature and all her gifts. We noticed, we saw the rebirth, we walked barefoot on the earth and frolicked in her bounty. I worry that many children do not know anymore what flowers grow in spring and when the full Pink Moon of April will rise.

We have a wedding here on the 17th. By here, I mean our backyard. Yes, I am a bit nervous, but I am happy and most importantly, Elizabeth and Erik are happy. We have dug deep into the interiors of this timeworn house finding antique linens from my mother-in-law, linens she set her

Passover table with decades ago and pieces of mismatched china to set our tables. We dug some more and discovered beautiful tablecloths with delicate embroidered spring flowers done by my grandma Farris and cloths with eyelet lace that dressed my mother's Thanksgiving tables for all my memory. We will use all for Elizabeth's wedding (thank you Tere for gently giving a beautiful new life to these old linens). We looked through my very simple wedding album and read the gifts I received in 1979, almond colored kitchen cannisters, 10-dollar checks and bath towel sets. We found a single unused wedding invitation and Elizabeth then found the similar paper to print hers on. We made lists and checked things off and we got uptight and then light again. I cried when we previewed the "Here Comes the Bride" song and when, at random moments, my sister Susan's name was mentioned. We found something blue, a bracelet from my Aunt Irene, and Elizabeth tried on my simple tea length wedding dress from Abdallas. Fresh cut flowers were ordered and will find their places in small glass vases on tables set in spring attire, (an advance "thank you" to Agnes for a beautiful flower display that will wondrously appear on April 17th). Guests will come from New England and Ville Platte and two will become one under the night sky in our backyard. She and I scurried around town and found so many people and places to help us put this together and many times, Elizabeth said how happy she was to be home to have her wedding here in New Iberia. And I have written before and I will write again, there's no place like home.

I wish you a happy Easter and last day of Passover. I hope you spot a baby dragonfly in your garden, and I hope you have the opportunity to make a clover flower necklace with a small child.

p.s. Concerning the asparagus fern I wrote about last month, I think it will not make it, but I will, and you will too.

May 30, 2021

Tiny and quiet as it was, it sheltered full-sized probing dreams of childhood for many of us. For me, the little blue building in the alleyway sandwiched between King's Office Supply and a bare brick structure next to the Sportsman Bar was where I imagined my art studio would be someday. Someday, I thought, when I came back from traveling and studying painting in France. I imagined I would go to southern France where van Gogh had packed canvases on his back, wet from oils and flaming from the Mediterranean sun, walking, painting, never knowing what would become of his work. He walked that land I dreamed of seeing. He walked and painted without much to sustain him, neither food nor much hope, in this magical place where cypress trees grew, and absinthe flowed, and the movement of natural light was noticed and placed on stretched canvases. That was my plan, that was my youthful wish, to see this faraway land and this "dream", this plan, somehow, included the curious little building in the alley. Well, not much of any of that unfolded. I did study painting in Nice France the summer between my junior and senior year at LSU and I did see Van Gogh's cypress trees from a window on a train to Florence, but I never made the little blue building my studio. And I suspect many never did what was imagined with the soon to be gone building either.

Dreams from youth, I still think of them sometimes, usually when seasons change, like now when the timidity of spring bursts into maturity, when there is high-volume buzz and penetrating color and more youthful dreams to fill the enchanting days of summer. Speaking of youth, I attended the

CHS graduation this year and watched eighty-four young people, including my nephew, Zac Farris, walk down the aisles of St. Peter's holding the honor of being the 100th graduating class from the original school, St Peter's College. Then, in 1922, there were only seven young men to receive diplomas from the newly formed school, now there are many more and many are girls. This piece of time, this tiny stretch, this deep pocket of thoughts right after high school is where dreams burst with possibilities, it is where "spring" turns to "summer", it is where life moves on.

My vantage point has become abruptly different now than when I walked down the aisle of St. Peter's Church in 1972. I reflect and know that most of the dreams I carried with me then were sparked from the people and places of this small town. Many are no longer here, both the people and the places, for time inevitably takes things away physically, and it is our hearts that we must rely on to keep them protected and remembered. I have written about it before and I mention it again, for I cannot think of my creative journey , my youthful aspirations, without thinking of The Cottage, an edifice of lofty dreams and creative travels with Mrs.Renoudet, the sweet lady who answered all of my questions about making art and the Halls of Carmel, where Mrs. Swatloski encouraged my journey into the arts and Sister Ann Carmel taught me how. These are my specific people and places I write about, but they can be interchanged by anyone reading this. The feelings are the same, the places we went in youth carry us to now. The weave of the small-town fabric is tight and bounding; it is made up of the teachers that saw things in us, the coaches that pushed, the small businesses that called us by our first names and knew our parents and the security of home. Small towns are rich with dream starters, they give our youth a secure launching pad and the stimulation and encouragement to follow their visions. They nurture dreams that may only find you on a train to Florence looking out of the window but then, through time, find you at a keyboard sharing the memories.

Congratulations to the graduates. I hope all of us here have given you a fertile ground to dream, the skills to carry them through and an honorable reason to remember this unique place called home ….you've "got the whole world in your hands".

June 27, 2021

In two days, I will be sixty-seven years old. This will be two years beyond my mother's life and nearly eight years beyond my sister's; it is a faceless interval for me. I do like it here, most days, for it is a place of shrewdness and abandonment. I suppose I compliment myself to proclaim I am "shrewd", but I am somewhat. So are you. If a person has lived for nearly seven decades and was paying attention, they know things; they are shrewd. And I use the word "abandonment" to describe myself in a positive context. I do not use it to imply I do not care anymore; I care, but only about people. I do not care about things. I have already traveled through those somewhat materialistic days of youth where everything looked shiny and new and desirable, and I partook. I do regret much of that accumulation, but I am happy it had a definite beginning and a sudden end. I am in a place now that I enjoy the challenge of not needing as many things.

I do not need to "fit in" either. I do not need to understand all that is going on, all the tumult of the world. I just need to accept myself and function as a good steward within my small space, a space where, at arm's length, I can possibly be of help and assistance to someone and I can make more of an effort to treat the natural world with concern; that's it, that is where I am at nearly sixty-seven. I feel as though I have somewhat successfully abandoned the judgement and intensities of the world, and, in exchange, I have found universal acceptance and a life lived closer to the Earth. Currently, I am in search of summer.

Sometimes I find it in the garage where the June bugs gather at night and where my bees look for a faint light, those that dare to leave the hive after dark. I find it when I hear thunder in the distance, and I run to my clothesline to quickly gather clothes. I see it when the cerulean sky fills with fluffy white clouds, puffs that were there in childhood when the green grass was something I laid on and found horses and sailboats and strange faces in the elusiveness of the sky.

Summer is there in the heat of the day when I hear the loudness of the locusts and the quietness of the neighborhood. I remember those moments in summer when I was a child, it was a time to come inside, and my mother would have a bologna sandwich and Kool-Aid for me. Sometimes she would cut the sandwich into two triangles and the Evangeline

Maid bread was soft and mounded with mayonnaise. The Kool - Aid was cold with ice was from an aluminum ice tray with a lever you pulled back to release the perfectly shaped cubes. "As the World Turns" was on the television and the unplanned afternoon stretched out forever; the world was as big and beautiful as my imagination.

I end this open letter of sorts with a humble and unsolicited suggestion; go outside. It is hot but you might see a brown lizard turning to green while perched on a daylily or a blue dragonfly with eyes big enough to see the real world. Go near a field and watch the winged hunters swoop down to catch their breakfast, watch as Nature balances itself. Watch and try not to disturb that balance, for the smallest part of Nature is important. Pick the herbs from your garden to hang and dry for your winter soups. Cut and gather fresh basil and go inside for a cool off and make a small batch of pesto; fill the kitchen with the smell of basil and tonight, cook pasta, add the pesto, and toss...

July 25, 2021

I feel as though I find the same warmth and peace amongst the spaces within my house and my yard that a baby finds in the face of its mother. It is where I most want to be these days, in my house and amongst the nature that surrounds it. I find comfort within the physical space that holds much of my life, this place where my children grew, where meals were prepared, flowers and trees were planted and where I paint and write. The walls of this house encapsulate the warmth of the memories and promise security in the days ahead; it is where much life is lived.

I have been blessed to see many different places in my life, many, sadly, no longer there. I have seen Armadillo World Headquarters in Austin Texas where Willie Nelson and Jerry Jeff Walker played on summer nights when Austin was gearing up to set a new "stage". I have seen NYC when it was big, dangerous and beyond the scope of my mind. I have visited the Uffizi Gallery in Florence without waiting in a line and into the Academie Gallery to see the David the same way. I have made a last-minute decision to walk into Tiger Stadium, just by showing my student id, to watch Charles McClendon's LSU Tigers play Bear Bryant's Crimson Tide. I have gone to the Emerald Coast and stayed in beach bungalows with windows open and breezes from the ocean rolling in. I have shopped with my grandparents at the French Market in New Orleans when fresh fruits and vegetables were loaded off boats that rolled down the Mississippi River and men from other lands unloaded wooden crates of melons and bananas. I have walked down Main Street in the evenings with my parents to "window shop" and I have sat through three consecutive showings of Viva Las Vegas at the Essanee Theater in 1964. One day, I feel certain, I will want to see more of the beauties the world has to show me, but now, in the middle of July in my 67th year ,I want to see home. Home, for me, is where the magic is.

Outside of my backdoor, the sounds of the Deep South in mid-summer are delightfully deafening, The noise is thunderous and the goings on are amazing...hens are clucking, bees are buzzing, dragonflies are searching, birds are singing and lizards are basking... I sometimes feel like I am inside of a Little Golden Book.

I have planted on this property for nearly thirty-seven years. It was barren in 1985 except for the nearby woods; my mom referred to our yard as "the desert". Now, it is home to so many small animals and insects. We have butterflies and caterpillars and dragonflies and all kinds of birds. And in the woods, there are racoons and opossums and snakes. At night, when the moon rises and the daytime noise ends, spiders weave their intricate, glorious webs and the chattering squirrels settle down. Then, the moon sets, the sun rises, and Nature wakes up once again. No matter what may be occurring in my life, she is outside of my door doing exactly what she does. She is always there for me to watch, to enjoy and to learn.

I write this to perhaps provoke enthusiasm in someone who is, as I, a big fan of Mother Nature and would like to help her out a bit. I promise, you will be rewarded. It's been many many years of cultivating, planting, feeding, and watering that has given me this joy I see today, this array of butterflies and honeybees and ladybugs and trees that bear fruit and flowers that give nectar and fragrance. Anyway, maybe my unpretentious message and simple words will be read by someone young, as I once was, and they will begin a garden or plant a tree or feed the birds. In doing so, they will begin to create a journey that will bring them joy throughout their lives and provide them with a shelter from some of their trials. They will create a place that becomes their favorite place, a place that is their magic.

I am going to be a grandmother….I am going to soon learn of this new level of love.

August 2021

I cleaned my paint brushes and then read some random article about the poisoning of the Earth, the poisoning with pesticides to grow potatoes on land that belonged to Native Americans. I did these two very diverse things before 5:30 in the morning. My brushes needed a good scrubbing, for they had helped me with a painting that brought me spiritual joy. It is a small painting, one of whimsy with a bit of fantasy and realism all mixed up together, much like this world we are in. In the faint light of the morning, I walked across the wooden floor of my studio to the kitchen sink with brushes that dripped of turpentine, not really caring, for the floor had been through the childhood of five children and, most recently, the pathway into our house for Elizabeth and Erik's outdoor wedding. The worn oak planks shamelessly sport paint stains and blemishes, much like I. I have grown to love its secret story and consequentially have little concern with its flawed veneer. So began this new day in the middle of August, in the seventh decade of my life. I have coffee now and I am writing, the clock just struck 6.

These two occurrences I mention unexpectedly set a direction for my day. I tried to pull them together, these two different and extreme situations that casually presented themselves to me in those mystic moments before sunrise, those moments where the adjustment of my day at hand somewhat formulates.

My day, this day in the middle of 2021, is a time of confusion, a time of much disarray. Sometimes, I feel this weight of the world and other times, I only see what is in front of me. We all have our places we "go to", places that adjust the balance and equilibrium of our thoughts and therefore our lives; I find that place in my garden.

I have recently moved toward a prairie sort of arrangement lately, a situation that grew from a deeper love of Nature and her natural beauty. I also know that if you fill your garden with native plants, the butterflies and the honeybees will come, they know the difference. My garden is an ongoing journey, it will never "get there", instead, it will evolve and change as my life does. One day I will be older, and it will be older too. I will not be as able to tend it and Mother Nature will have a heavier hand. I will have to allow that. It may be that I am enjoying the natural state more because somehow, I know that later in my life it will be different.

The swallowtails, monarchs, dragonflies, the wild bunnies from the woods and my honeybees are all welcome here in this space that is only a small part of the world, but it is mine to share with all that come (except maybe the squirrels; they are eating my pecans, ha). I have written so many hundreds of heartfelt words, so many itemized descriptions about Nature; this one, however, is somewhat of an indirect plea. We can all be kinder; we can all give something back to her.

That's it, that's how I adjust this contemporary world in my mind. I can hardly do much to solve the global problems, but I can tend to the small circle I exist in, and I can do my best to make it better. I can be kind to the earth and to my neighbor and I can grow food for my family and lastly, I can feed my spirit.

I share my simple morning ritual with you and extend this concerning thought in hope that you find a place of peace and charity within these days ahead, these days of uncertainty.

When we all do a little, it will all help a lot.

September 2021

It seems the days roll in quickly, they roll in and roll out sometimes without even telling me. The next day, I wonder, what did I even do yesterday? It's all so fast and it keeps getting faster. I thought when I retired from teaching, my days would coil around the hours much slower. I thought I would find idle time here and there and early morning walks and late afternoon writing or painting while a soup was simmering for supper or a leftover casserole heating in the oven. That did not happen. It's Monday and then, it's Sunday. I am perplexed and I try to "fix" it because I do want slow, not slow to the point of non-productivity, but slow to the point of complete absorption.

I remember when my children were little, when time did seem kinder. They were keen observers of their environment; they had time to "absorb". I always suspected it was because they were physically low to the ground, and they saw the part of life that was important and miraculous. They saw the kingdom of creatures that scurried and hopped and flew and crawled and ate and built, there in the soil and in the grass. Their small hands touched all that they could catch, and their bare feet walked across the warm earth, whether it was soggy or dry and time was theirs and it was slow. Technology was not a thief then, there was the natural world to discover and learn from; there was only truth. The sky did not lie, it let them know when the clouds were full of moisture and would soon drop rain onto the earth. The trees did not sway them wrong; they wore tiny buds of green when spring was coming and leaves of gold in autumn. The small animals scurried each day just like the days before, foraging for food, always looking onward for fear of an enemy. Frogs came out in the rain and mockingbirds aggressively ruled the activity in the oak trees, sadly, chasing the Bluebirds away. They picked berries in late spring, sometimes dug potatoes in June, carved pumpkins for Halloween and made pinecone turkeys for the Thanksgiving table. It was all real and it was what consumed our days then. Now, the distractions are so abundant and accessible; they sometime stab us in the gut. It is more and more difficult to avoid the constant pounding of this phenomena we call "social media". Like all things, some of it is good but much of it is a distraction from the things that "really" are good.

The autumn moon will be full this Monday and Wednesday will herald in the first day of fall. For most of my life, fall was signaled by the Sugarcane Festival. When I was little, it meant sweater weather was approaching and the Ferris wheel could be seen over the treetops in City Park. The art show was setting up in the armory and stalks of sugarcane and favorite recipes were on display in the basement of the Sugarcane Festival Building. On Friday, the whole town dressed up like farmers, donning straw hats, overalls from Broussard Brothers, boots from Gulottas and red bandannas from the dime store. The 4 Hers were in the livestock shed caring for their animals, Main Street was roped off for a fais do do and all the downtown businesses were decorated with stalks of cane. It was a proud celebration of rural descent; it was the harvest. The full moon would appear to light the nighttime fields and the cooler air rolled in to give us a reason to make gumbo. The picture of the new Queen Sugar would be in the Sunday paper as well as a long list of the "winners" in the art and food competition. Much hometown pride and merriment were injected into the lives of most all the townspeople during this last weekend of September, the month that was the prelude to the "Holidays", beginning with Halloween and ending on the Epiphany. Anyway, times have changed and much of the above is different now. But the biggest difference of all is having to cancel the festival once more. I extend a humble newsprint "thank you" to our farmers that plow the earth to give us the food we need. Technology is now a huge part of that industry also, but the major component, the earth, is still beneath their feet and in their hands.

October 2021

It seems there is an Indian Summer happening here. The woods are changing, and the leaves are falling but the crisp coolness of Autumn is slow to arrive. I somehow knew October would come quickly, it always does, this little fleeting pocket of the year I love. This place where I hear the mill from my backyard and the slow-moving trusty tractors filled to the brim with sweet stalks of cane are up ahead on the backroads, roads I have traveled for most of my life. These are the sights and sounds of home. The days are shorter now and waiting for the full Hunter Moon to hang from the sky, overlooking the fields, giving more light for the farmers.
The gold and purple wildflowers are covering the meadows and ditches and the last of the summer butterflies are hovering over late summer zinnias and pentas. Full grown lizards

and dragonflies are scurrying in these last days of warm weather; they know cooler weather is ahead, just as the squirrels know and just as the trees know to take in the remaining chlorophyll stored in their leaves; all the living things are preparing for winter, all are scampering in this Indian Summer, for winter is near. It seems like it was yesterday when it was spring and I would sometimes find butterflies and lizards as babies, showing up unexpectedly in the garden, tiny little gifts from nature that had the seemingly insurmountable task of growing and staying alive throughout the summer months. Many of them did; the dragonflies lit on my clothesline when I was hanging sheets in mid-July and the lizards scurried along the deck banister hunting and growing. I see only a few now and these few have made it...the bugs of summer are changing with the season.

The seasonal tilt of the planet causes a new and interesting cast of light in my house. From the color and the outdoor beauty of October, I walk into a scattering of light, inside light that is beautiful and wonderous. I have ample "normal" light from electricity, but the miraculous light of the sunrise and sunset is there also, the spiritual lights that flow through crystal prisms in the morning and disperse through my keeping room window in the early evening, magical sunbeams that find their way inside. It is as though I have a beautiful and restoring visitor each day and for thirty-five years, I have made it a point to welcome this dance across these rooms, this dance that makes me feel happiness, happy that the natural world has no interest in the noise of the world.

As a final note, with nothing to do about the season but with everything to do with life and how you live it, I ask, "How do you make civics class interesting"? My answer would be to have Lawrence Narcisse Jr. teach it. Mr. Narcisse is one of the teachers I have remembered through all my life with admiration. It was 1969 in a classroom in New Iberia High School. I was a timid freshman sitting in this somewhat new and huge school in a potentially boring Civics class. Our teacher was this young, meticulously dressed in a suit, tie and polished dress shoes, man armed with knowledge and an obvious love of teaching. He stood in front of the classroom of wide eyed fourteen-year-olds and explained the three branches of government. He was accomplished and well prepared, a teacher that was, by anyone's stringent standard, a role model, someone who obviously loved his profession and was there to enlighten and inspire young minds and he did.

I read recently that he has passed. I write this to acknowledge that I still remember his engaging Civics Class, and, because of him, I have a decent understanding of the importance the three branches of government are to our country. Thank you, Mr. Narcisse for a job well done. I include you in a list of teachers who taught their students "how" to think, to gather the facts, deliberate and make our own "educated" decisions; he did that.

Until next month, have a spooky Halloween, lookup in the sky Wednesday to see the Full Hunter Moon, be thankful for our farmers, and find a way for your harvest to be "enough".

November 2021

I was caught outside one morning when the front blew in. I had consolidated my hens the night before and was checking on their transition. Winter is coming and tending to one coop is brutal enough during the icy mornings, so they have to all live together during the colder months. Sorry chicks, but that's the rules here. Anyway, for those of you who do not keep chickens, they are not okay with new members entering their flock. "Birds of a feather flock together" is a truism in the chicken world. Because of this and because chickens are not very "scholarly", I always move new hens into the coop with the previous hens during the night when the chickens are somewhat blind and, therefore, not aware, otherwise, the "pecking order" becomes an issue and some may not survive. The next morning, hopefully, the new hens are just part of the group, and everyone gets along. That's what I was doing when the wind became a North wind, blowing leaves and hinting at a forthcoming chill; the front had arrived, summer was over. The cool wind was welcome, but it blew in a small gust of melancholy, as it always does.

With the fronts, come the holiday season, the first one being Thanksgiving, and with the holiday season, comes a potpourri of emotions, most of them are joyful but some, are reflective. The latter is a focus of this piece.

It seems as though I can smell the hint of sage in my Grandma Farris' cornbread dressing and anticipate Tom Turkey will soon sit on the special white platter in the center of my mother's table as she stands next to the Thanksgiving feast in her holiday apron tensely watching my dad unwillingly, but skillfully, tackle the carving of the celebrated Bird. This iconic, Norman Rockwell event happened year after year. I suppose I thought it would never end; they would always be there in the Thanksgiving kitchen laughing, talking, hugging my babies, and feeding turkey and creamed potatoes to my small children, but as you know, nothing is forever.

This is, for many of us, the time of year when everyone special in your life enters your physical space and vividly enters your memory. By the time you reach my age, there are, unfortunately, a few empty seats at the symbolic table. But the holidays are good, they are the catalyst that intensifies our memories from times past and welcomes us to openly recall, to share stories and actively include everyone we love in our circle of life, past and present. The holidays are an invitation to remember. We, once again, for a short moment, are enclosed in a circle of rich memory and love, thankful for all that are here and thankful for time spent with and the memory of those who are not.

As in nature, with the falling leaves of autumn, come a few falling tears as the North winds blow, causing us to remember days gone by. Along the wisps of the breeze, however, there is exultation for the approaching celebrations and hope and energy for the new year ahead. Though sad to see the bareness on the trees and in our lives, there beneath our feet are wonderous colors, beautiful acts of God to celebrate the season and to enjoy, as life unfolds in yet, another way.

Pull out your grandma's cornbread dressing recipe, the one with the butter smudges and deep creases, make your sister's rice dressing, wear your mother's tattered apron, think of them, talk about them and keep them nearby.

Best wishes at Thanksgiving to all of you who follow my Sunday column. For that, I am especially thankful. Be happy...the people that love you, wish that for you.

December 2021

The small fireplace was in the living room at 111 Beech Street; it was a place of wonder for a child. There were fifteen of us then, fifteen first cousins, that, throughout childhood, sat near there, that toasted sliced bread there and huddled on the cold mornings of winter when we spent the night. It was in my mammae's house, a house from long ago, a house where my mother and her four siblings grew up, a house where pieces of my childhood quietly unfolded, a house I will never forget.

It is Christmas time once again and as Dickens so shrewdly wrote, Christmas Past will come to visit. His visit finds me in this cozy space in Ville Platte, Louisiana in the nineteen sixties. The world was, as it is now again, in much upheaval…. times were changing. But, on Beech Street, time was cozy, time was still, time was now, in this old house with my Mamae Daire. She seemed old then, but really, she wasn't, she had just been through many trials of life. She was born in 1904 in rural Evangeline Parish, her family name was Soileau. She would marry Lester Daire and together they would have 5 wonderful children, one being my mother, Mary Nella Daire. When she was 38, her husband suddenly died. The family had moved into town by then, they had left the farm, the mulberry tree, the prairie and moved into a little white house on Beech Street.

At the time of her husband's passing, her first language was French, World War II was upon them, and her children ranged in age from 5 to 18 years. I have many stories from my mother of these times; she was 9 years old. These times that everyone in our country suffered in some way or another, these times of fighting for our freedoms, these times of rations and guns and death and sorrow and eventually victory, victory won with many battle scars. But, by 1962, despite the hardships from the past, there were layers of happy days in that little white house.

There was a cow and a fig tree in the backyard and a China Ball tree to climb in the front yard. There was Steen's syrup on the table and a party line running through the old black phone. Everyone spoke French and laughed and hugged and loved one another...that's what I remember.

Back to the fireplace...so much happened there. In the years before, my mother sat near it to warm her hands before going off to school or work and it kept the house and the Daire children a little warmer on winter nights. Now, it was a place of enchantment where we, the cousins, listened for little chimney swifts that might be trapped in the flue and toasted bread for a snack, white bread dangling off the prongs of a fork held near the fire to toast. This tiny fireplace seemed like Christmas to me, it seemed as though Santa had magically come down the impossibly small chimney years ago when my mother was little, and might he come again?

I do not have many "real" Christmas memories there, however. I 49 was not built yet and travel was not as ordinary then. I do, however, remember one Christmas when there was a small tree in a corner and 15 loosely wrapped presents. My mammae had gone to "the store" (which was really a neighbor's house on the corner that "accommodated" a one room general store) and bought a small and modest gift for each of us. My gift was little pink soaps in a decorative glass bottle. I still have that glass bottle in the attic and her little white house on Beech Street in my heart. It was all so simple; it was all so real and lasting.

Take from this piece what you like, but mostly, take from it the spirit.
Christmastime is about those tiny moments. Christmas, in its purest sense, requires no money, it only requires love and a "fireplace" to keep you warm throughout the years of your life.

January 2022

I begin this first column of the new year by saying "thank you" for continuing to read my Sunday musings. This January begins my sixteenth year of submissions to our hometown paper. Morris Raphael began this space in the Daily Iberian with his weekly column, Bayou Browsing. He wrote of events and happenings around town, both past and present, with decorum and expertise. I am totally humbled to have contributed, albeit very different from his content to the Daily Iberian and its readers for this moment in time.

The new year tiptoed in with humidity, mosquitos and red geraniums blooming profusely at my back door. It was an odd start of winter with curses of covid lurking, horrific fires in Colorado and Lafayette, Louisiana and red tomatoes on a renegade tomato plant that emerged from a compost heap. My hens, sort of, knew it was December though, they mostly quit laying as the winter equinox emerged and the days became shorter...they understood. But much of nature seemed confused with warm weather and air conditioners on and people last minute Christmas shopping in shorts. It was odd.

I think about nature always and write about it often; it is both my sanctuary and my concern. While I have no scientific background or education in the matter, I am, and have been for all my life, an observer, dare I say, a keen observer. I worry about the decreasing habitats for our wildlife and the normalization of the heavy use of chemicals in our food supply, while I appreciate the colossal challenge to supply housing and food for our ever-growing population.

I do know that all the above comes with a price to our environment. Anyway, as I said, I am not qualified to be more than an observer…I have no solution, therefore I have no effective "voice". I can, however, take good care of my small space, I can try to be a better steward. In this new year, I plan to grow more of my own food, plant only native, leave the meadow, leave the leaves, consume less, and be more aware. It is only me and something small but as Pete Seeger once wrote, "The world will be solved by millions of small things".

While I am in this somewhat of a "negative" slant with this writing, and I apologize for this adverse vibe, I would like to interject something positive…we all have a lovely small town in which to live and raise our families and spend our energy and time. I am writing this at the beginning of 2022 to appeal to all who may be reading this, to do the small things to make our space on this gigantic sphere work in harmony, to make it the best it can be, to be the solution to a problem that is before you. There are numerous names I could list here that are committed to doing just that, community conscious people that are trying to make our hometown the best it can be. I appreciate their efforts, I hope to also be, however small, a contributor, not a complainer…that is my new year's resolution. To quote Pete Seeger again, "It's been my belief that learning how to do something in your hometown is the most important thing."

The Full Wolf Moon will rise on January 17.and, on January 13, Skip and I may have a grandson; I may discover another chamber of my heart that houses even more love than I knew possible. I may discover, yet another reason, to take care of all that I can, to do my tiny part to make the whole a better place. Best wishes for 2022…bloom where you are planted and, perhaps, plant where you live.

March 2022

I walked in the woods this morning. I wanted to greet Spring properly. She was there, just beginning her arrival into our hemisphere, just beginning to gently push aside the cold barrenness of winter and give to us the promise of new life. The first thing I thought of on my walk into our woods was my tiny new grandson, Santiago. I imagined how fun it will be years from now to take him here, walking and discovering, new life meeting new life, what could be better?

My woods are small, only about three acres, but they are untouched. Nature does her thing here, small trees fall and provide housing for many creatures as they decompose and feed the fertile soil, birds and the wind plant saplings, families of rabbits and squirrels and birds and frogs are born and live and thrive here in this refuge where there is no threat of gunfire or traps or poison. Fireflies, dragonflies, and honeybees live freely, and they help to pollinate the forest and my nearby garden. And one day, my grandson will be here to see it all, just as his dad did.

Next to the woods, is a field and our yard. The wildflowers are beginning to show off their beauty and provide nectar for my bees. The dandelions have been here for a bit, and some are displaying their stout yellow flowers. The seemingly simple dandelion provides nectar for the bees and are the precursor for childhood wishes, for their seed "bubbles" just "ask" to be blown.

And when I look up, I see the clear blue sky and new buds against it and as I walk, I hear the rustle of something of the earth, something that scurries to get out of my way not knowing he is safe. The baby bunnies are still beneath the ground, but soon, I will catch sight of the mother bunnies in my garden, and I will, once again, understand the annoyance of Peter Rabbit and the plight of Farmer McGregor. The bluebirds will soon sail across the meadows and baby lizards will begin to bask on my wooden fence. The spring peepers are beginning to mate and if you listen, you can hear them late in the evening. St. Patrick's Day is on the seventeenth and the Full Worm Moon will rise on the eighteenth. It is all so wonderous and astonishing, this rebirth.

These things all happen no matter what is going on in the world of humans, Mother Nature is steadfast. I find solace in knowing this, knowing that she is there yet another day, another season to share her gifts with all of us, no matter what.

Little by little like a mouse eating an elephant, I will get the early spring work done. I will paint the bee boxes, plant zinnia seeds, pot geraniums and amend the garden. As I do, I will grow stronger, both physically and spiritually. I will hear the birds and listen carefully to the sound of the new season coming in and be thankful that I am a small part of it and wish on a dandelion, that all people of the world could celebrate this new beginning.

April 2022

It seemed as though the air was so pure then. In early spring, my mom would open the windows and her little homemade muslin curtains would wave when the wind blew and the screens kept out the mosquitos and let the birdsong in, birdsong from the woods that surrounded us, us, our young family, in 1962. I was eight, my sister, Susan, was four and my baby brother, Dwayne, was only six weeks old when we moved to Little Woods. It was the beginning of a new neighborhood, a space to live, grow up in, carved from woods far away from town and near the Bayou Teche. We had a star route address, and our phone number was Emerson 40757. Mr.

Curtis Oubre, bus 21, was our bus driver and the few children that lived in Little Woods had to walk to the main highway to catch the bus. He always wore a hat and had a friendly smile. It was a lovely time and place to be a child.

In spring, my mom would scatter marigold seeds in the front of the house in a little flower bed my dad turned over with a shovel. She watered until the seeds sprouted and grew; I still remember the strong smell the tiny flowers made. I always include them in my garden, and I think of her. Honeysuckle grew wild on the broken barbed wire fence that separated our house from a thicket, a thicket that made way to a pasture where brown eyed cows grazed, and a garden grew. Trips to town were few in 1962. "Town" was far away, and we didn't really need much. My mom cooked each day, and she made brownies, jello and banana pudding for our snacks. Every weekday, after work, my dad would call her to ask if she needed anything from the grocery store. Usually, it was a loaf of Evangeline Maid bread or a gallon of milk. Shortly after we moved there, Pelican Creamery started delivering and life was easier, but my dad still called. The Pelican Creamery delivery man would come into our kitchen, open our refrigerator, and fill it with Borden's milk, ice cream, and eggs. Imagine.

We lived through Hurricanes Hilda (1964) and Betsy (1965), in that house when all we had was a transistor radio and KANE AM. I can remember when the news announcer on KANE signed off during one of those storms right before "the eye" was expected to hit New Iberia, "This is KANE 1240 signing off, good night and good luck" ...it was a moment of tremendous vulnerability.

Anyway, I write this to remember but also to realize how much has changed since those seemingly simpler days. I suppose we all look back and label our youth as the "good ole days", time has a way of softening the hardships and heartaches that occurred then. But as I try to be honest, I still think those days were good. Those days of the security of home where, no matter what happened during the day, home was a place to go to and your world would be put right-side up again. The world was big, and your imagination took you to places in the woods and places far far away. There was a tree to climb, supper at the table, and marigolds in the front yard.

Easter Sunday is near, and as I have written before, Easter is the first Sunday after the first full moon (the Paschal Full Moon) after the spring equinox. This year the Full Pink Moon will rise on the 16th and Easter Sunday will follow on the 17th.

I wish all of you the opportunity and desire to create memories in spring that will reach far into the future and become someone's "soft place to land".

May 1, 2022

I do not remember everything, but I remember the important things about my mother. I remember the routine, but caring way, she peeled potatoes, standing in the kitchen near the sink, as I sat at the small wooden table, and we talked as she prepared supper. We talked about everything. I remember the way she blotted her red lipstick with tissue and the way she dabbed perfume behind her ear. I can barely recall her at my graduation or wedding, for those were such big events and anxiety took most of those memories, but I remember her in an ordinary day, preparing supper for her family, sitting at the kitchen table having a cup of coffee as she listened and then dispelled all the troubles of my world. I remember the pan of homemade chocolate brownies she baked from her old Betty Crocket Cookbook, the one she received as a wedding gift in June of 1952, and I remember (and still have) the black and white check apron with embroidered flowers on the pockets that she wore to prepare Thanksgiving dinner. I remember the way she made a pin curl with a baby Elizabeth's hair and pinned it with a bobby pin from hers, and the way she loved my boys.

There were so many ordinary days with her, summer days when I was a child coming in the house with blackberries I had scoured the woods for. She would stop all she was doing and put together a small cobbler. I will never forget the taste and the happiness I felt. She knew to grab those moments, to make those childhood memories for us, for that, is what would remain. The big moments are wonderful, but they can be laced with anxiety and confusion: those little moments are the real jewels…. she knew that.

Spring is settling in here, the intense heat is lurking, and the mosquitoes will soon be crashing all our outdoor events. But today is the first day of May, and for me, no day can hardly be lovelier; the entire month delivers so much beauty. The magnolias are beginning to bloom and scenting the air, a fragrance that reminds me of my mom, for one was nearly always in a jar sitting on the kitchen counter spilling its seeds and scenting the kitchen with the faintness of lemon. The shrubs in my flower beds are beginning to whisper in May, for the tiny lizards and garden snakes are grown now and scurry as I walk past them on the sidewalk. Our gardens are planted, giving us hope for a rich summer harvest…fresh tomatoes for our sandwiches and salads, peppers to sauté, cucumbers to slice and eggplant to bake. The fig trees are covered in beautiful big leaves, sheltering the tiny fruit in somewhat of a futile attempt to keep the birds away, for their fruit becomes their seeds and their seeds assure new life. The dewberries and mulberries are abundant this year and ready to be picked to eat fresh with a sprinkle of sugar or to make jams and jellies or spur-of-the-moment cobblers. The Full Flower Moon will rise in the middle of this magnificent month to shine over fields of flowers and, hopefully, that night will be clear, and we will see, once again, the infinite beauty of Mother Nature.

I extend early Happy Mother's Day wishes to all, to moms of new babies that make sleep a challenge, to moms of "stimulating" teens, to moms of grown children, to moms of fur babies, and to the special moms that are caretakers of those in need. Happy Mother's Day to all that nurture. I also offer a gentle (unsolicited) reminder; our children are watching, and their fabric is from the bolt that is you. It is a beautiful and unique gift; but it comes with a responsibility, the greatest responsibility of all.

May 29, 2022

It is difficult to put pleasant words on paper right now. It is difficult to focus on the beauty of Spring and the peacefulness of May, the month where nature calms down a bit and gives us time in our gardens and time to sit on porches and swings and have enchanting visions of the summer ahead; it is perhaps impossible to write about that now. My mother's heart, as is yours, is heavy from the suffering in Uvalde; I cannot put what happened there in a place I can understand.

I remember being in that area many years ago when I was in college. I knew someone from that part of Texas, Del Rio, Uvalde, the Rio Grande. I traveled there a few times; it was a fascinating place; it was a place so unlike here. It was my image of Texas, tumble weeds, mesquite trees, beautiful sunsets, and people that had lived there forever. While it was a physically harsh environment, it was enchanting. The population, of course, was much smaller in 1975 but I am suspecting the demographics were much the same. I remember going into Acuna Mexico, Del Rio's border town, without any hassle, we just crossed over, had dinner, walked around and reentered Texas. I was 21 years old and probably oblivious to anything beyond my immediate scope and the socialization occurring in my life but my recall of crossing the border is somewhat uneventful and I do not remember being fearful or anxious. Anyway, all of that was long ago and much has happened there and everywhere by now, some things incredibly good and some incredibly bad…the occurrence in Uvalde is the latter. The pain is bottomless, and the questions have no answers...

I have tried for sixteen and a half years to put pleasant and positive thoughts on this little space of newsprint that is my Sunday column and for the most part, I have been successful. There were a few columns about hurricanes such as Katrina and Ida that have darkened the tone and the oil spill in 2010 was a bummer, but, mostly, I have been blessed with positive prompts from mother nature, fond occurrences from our town and my memories that were somewhat, at least I hope, uplifting and positive, but today, I struggle.

I had planned to tell you how easy it is in summer to find and enjoy the little things in life, the small miracles that happen early in the morning right outside your backdoor and how easy it is to get into a sense of peace when the summer sun sets, and the evening air cools down with the sound of tree frogs and night birds in the distance. I wanted to tell you how wonderful the approaching summer will be with children off from school and vacations at the beach.

And I do still hope all the above happens in your life, in your summer, but, as it does, we should all hold in our hearts the families of Uvalde and do our parts, whatever that may be, to make this world kinder and safer for our children.

I end with a thought, a humble suggestion made without presumption or political undertone. Before casting blame and spewing contempt, before taking part in this great divide, try instead to use that energy to do something positive within your community, within your own family, that might be a more beneficial piece to this ailing puzzle.

June 2022

Some days, like yesterday, I think I will give up the garden and visit the farmer's market more often. I think I will leave all the work behind and, instead, buy from those who do it so well, the backyard gardener, the one I see from the road while driving by, the one with the old straw hat and long-sleeved shirt orchestrating an aesthetic masterpiece. He spends his day there, battling bugs, tying tomatoes, turning over peas for nitrogen, encouraging bees and ladybugs, and staying close to the earth. I want to be that person; I am, in my soul, but I do get discouraged. Anyway, I think of quitting when I am finding ways to scale down and simplify – the catch phrase of the decade –

I think about having more time to stop and rest, but then I go outside in the very early morning and the peppers have plumped up from the rain, the sun begins to shine but is still timid and kind, the dragonflies and monarchs hoover and light on the tiny white blooms of my pepper plants and, suddenly, my garden is so beautiful and giving. I pick a few cucumbers to go with lunch and a zucchini to make a dessert bread later in the day and a small bunch of zinnias for color. There are herbs for sauces and squashes and peppers and melon vines with promise and all my practical sense has banished, once again. "We come from the earth, we return to the earth, and in between we garden."

I wrote this journal entry ten years ago in June of 2012. It is still true today. Every year, somewhere in late June, I am a very disheartened gardener. This year the bugs and extreme temperatures have been my nemesis. However, as in each summer of my life, I have learned something in my garden, something to perhaps, make the next year better. Mother Nature is a steadfast teacher; she always has a lesson. Her knowledge is infinite, and the garden is one of her most artistic schoolrooms.

Despite the weather and the bugs, my kitchen counter is somewhat colorful with small tomatoes and medium sized cucumbers and my tiny vases near my sink are readily stocked with zinnias, just as my summer kitchen has always been. It does, however, seem more difficult this summer; it seems Mother Nature is in some sort of fury and her extreme heat is the manifestation. I suppose there will be some sort of adjustment. I know there is an attempt at compensation for my fig trees are "loaded" as are my citrus trees; life gives, and it takes, it wanes and waxes just like the moon.

I do not know any of what the future holds, for it seems life is more uncertain now than before; the world is a big, amplified cosmos of unsettlement and I am fearful at times. I do know that, if I am able, next spring, I will plant my garden and in late June, I will grumble about the heat and the bugs and think about it being my last, but then, I will see someone in a garden, a garden with rows of promise and goodness wearing an old straw hat and a long-sleeved shirt and I will fall in love once more.

July 2022

In the fall of 1969, a group of teenage girls were preparing for the dawning of the "Age of Aquarius". It was, once again, time for the Sophomore Hop to take place in the old Mt. Carmel Gym and the theme of the dance would be centered around that song. Some of the girls worked diligently on the construction of a giant size sun, a prop that would embody the coming of the Age of Aquarius. This "sun" and all the other homemade cardboard creations had a job to do; they had to make our night, our dance, dreamlike; and they did.

I mention this long-ago event for two reasons. First, I heard the Fifth Dimension sing this song on the 60s satellite station today and second, these girls I mention, me included, will be celebrating their fifty-year class reunion this fall; these two incidents collided and landed in my Sunday column.

Five decades of life have passed since the 1972 graduating class of MCA left that small world of security and fifty-three years have gone by since the Sophomore Hop with the giant sun taking center stage in an old gym that leaned. I remember those years and that school fondly. It was a place where classes started with prayer, brown plaid skirts were measured for (exact) length, Saturday demerits were given and every school day, Sr. Rose Marie "was on the Box"; it was a world so small and so safe and looking back, so magical. It was a place to launch, a place where we were encouraged to follow our dreams and the Golden Rule. It was a world where I truly believed when:

"Jupiter aligns with Mars

Then peace will guide the planets

And love will steer the stars."

I believed that with my entire 17-year-old heart. It seems the part about Jupiter aligning with Mars did come true on May 29, 2022; I'm just not so sure about the rest of the song.

It seems I have spent most of July canning figs; the harvest was abundant this year.

Have you ever felt so connected as standing under a sprawling LSU Purple fig tree fed by compost and grown to maturity with the half-moon overhead watching and the locusts' sounds getting louder with the dimming of the day? It was a great mid-summer moment I will take with me into the upcoming winter.

And my honeybees have had a great summer also. The worker bees are finding it difficult to keep the hive cool, but I feel certain they are filling their "pantry" with plenty of honey to last them the winter, for the flowers have been plentiful and their nectar generous this summer. Soon, Skip and I will put on our bee gear and hopefully take (only) our share of honey from the hives, an annual event that is so connected to nature, so basic and necessary. I am grateful for the bounty that nature has provided.

Next time I write we will be nearing the end of summer. Everyone will have returned from the beach and the mountains and wherever else your summer adventures have taken you. Until then, I hope to continue to see the clear night sky, the full-grown lizards basking while their baby lizards are scurrying around, somewhat lost in this new world and I hope to continue to share my clothesline with giant dragon flies and perhaps see the fat green garden snake once again. The full moon will rise on a night in August as we settle into another school year. I wish for our student's school dances with cardboard suns, dreams as far as their imaginations take them, and the opportunity to learn and thrive in innocence and safety. And for all of us, I wish a way to "Let the sunshine in".

August 21, 2022

The sights and sounds of the Deep South in mid-August are changing. The spectrum of color the prisms make are different now. They are still hanging in the same places in my windows, but somehow, their display is different; the earth is preparing for the arrival of the next season, another cloak to cover us in, another time to enjoy.

My summer house that I wrote about earlier is no longer; it is waning like the gibbous moon. The sun is setting at a different time and slightly different place so the shadows it makes inside are changing, moving into the autumn light. If I squint my eyes just a bit, I can see a slight amber cast in the early evening making the house seem cozier somehow. This old house and I will soon be ready for the fires of winter and the tightly closed windows with shades down to keep the heat in, shedding its summer vibrancy for the more somber tones of warmth. It will become a place I do not want to leave, a place where it is warm, a place to settle in and rest. At least, that's what I imagine, for this summer has given us extreme circumstances and I do feel weary from it.

Outside, the signs of change are not as subtle as before, they are showing up under the Tallow trees that are dropping yellow leaves after an active season of hanging their bright green tassels for my bees. And the animals are different; they have gone through another summer cycle and those that have made it are bigger from the bounty and slower from the late season heat; I think they too are ready to cool down and live in their autumn house. The black berry briars are a hostile place for the wrens and sparrows now, for the soft safe green foliage is gone and while the zealous mockingbirds still dominate the oak trees, the bluebirds have left the fields and pastures. The locusts continue to be somewhat deafening, but even they are getting tired; we are all somewhat weary from the heat and the endless rain; it is about "time for a cool breeze".

The end of summer, however, is just as lovely and animated as its beginning. Our backyards are brimming with the growth from the summer season; it is apparent in both our plants and in the insect world, everyone and everything has been busy these past months eating the earth's bounty and taking in the sunshine. If you garden, I suppose you are still cutting okra and if you have plenty, I assume you are smothering it to freeze, and one winter day, you will pull it out and put it in a chicken and sausage gumbo.

The bugs have, by now, taken over what is left from my summer garden and the rains have encouraged the ants to move on to the higher ground of my weed covered rows. I give up, I'm done. I saw the first sugarcane tractor yesterday and I am seeing ads for Sugarcane Festival T Shirts and events; we are about to feel festive in Iberia parish.

Anyway, this is my formal farewell to summer. Thank you for your bounty and thank you for the harvest that will soon be, but as they say, "Don't let the door hit you on the way out." Isn't it funny how the seasons are timed just right; it is as though someone knew how much of each we can allow and enjoy before it is time to anticipate and, ultimately, enjoy the next one.

September 4, 2022

Heat, humidity, endless rain, mosquitoes, inflation, politics...that about sums it up these days. But it is September now and a wonderful time of year is upon us. It begins with the "Festival", then the Gumbo Cook Off, a myriad of cruciferous vegetables at the farmers market, a cool snap, Halloween, Thanksgiving, Christmas, Hanukah, and all that is in between. I choose to focus more on these happy events and less on the abovementioned.

I never tire of the anticipation, the buzz, that begins here in September. We wait for the first "ever so slight" northern breeze while keeping our fingers crossed and saying our prayers that the Gulf remains calm until December 1. By now, our freezers are full of shrimp from the Gulf and smothered okra from our gardens. The gumbo pots are scrubbed clean and eager to christen the first gumbo of the season. The first tiny puff of cool morning air will become the news of the day. The mill on Northside Road will soon be turned on and Western boots will be on the shelves at Gulotta's. There will be a Fais do do under the Pavilion, carnival rides in the Plaza and a new Queen Sugar will be crowned…sounds like something from a Lifetime or Hallmark movie, doesn't it? This is us; this is what we do, this is what makes us a community.

The Full Harvest Moon will rise on September 10 setting the stage for all mentioned. This full moon is named the Harvest Moon because it is the full moon closest to the Autumnal Equinox on September 22. The Harvest Moon reminds us that summer is over, and the harvest begins. It rises soon after sunset, giving the farmers time to harvest their crops late into the evening. Best wishes to all our farmers for an abundant harvest.

I end with the following fragmented observation I wrote a few years ago and found on my computer while attempting to clean up some files...it seemed poignant enough to provoke a bit of leisure thought...

"I did not plan this, but I was outside at just the right time to take a very telling picture. It was a portrait of a sad, but true story about dominance and perhaps an example of Darwinism. I have kept chickens for possibly 25 years, and I have learned so much from these fabulous fowls; I could literally write a chapter's worth. For example, I now know that birds of a feather do flock together. I have learned that there is a definite hierarchy within each flock and if there is more than one rooster, as in my case and the point of this story, a dominant rooster will emerge. The rooster in the foreground is THAT rooster. He has already "eradicated" one other rooster, a delightful somewhat timid rooster with colorful tail feathers. His life was taken one day in a very graphic and brutal way. I was very sad, for he was the "underdog" of the barnyard and was the one rooster that seemed to "like" me; he was never aggressive towards me, hence his demise. There is another "outranked" rooster that remains; he has learned not to go near the hens or THAT rooster. I must feed him separately and, at night, he sleeps in the orange trees instead of in the safe coop. Sometimes, a small flock of hens will break away and hang out with him for a while but, mostly, he lives a life of solitude most always in fear."

I could go on and on about the things I have learned from my chickens…they have revealed natural traits in a raw and real way, traits and tendencies that are evident in all the natural world, some even within the human species…at least, that is my observation and accompanying opinion.

October 16, 2022

This will be a column filled with metaphors and doubts...

I have lived in the same house for thirty-seven and a half years. It sits on nearly eight acres, and it is my favorite place to be, but...it has outgrown me. Let me first proclaim, I hope to never leave this place, this place I where planted each tree, this place I chose every color for each wall, this place where Santa and the Tooth Fairy consistently visited and this kitchen that was always open, this place where I raised my family. It is where I want to be, it is my shelter and my home.

Now that I am much older than my house, we have both changed, a lot, and it has become a curious and challenging relationship. It seems my gardens and yard have not followed my lead; they have not slowed down like I am trying to do. Instead, they are growing profusely without consideration for the extra care they require! I cannot keep up. All the seeds, plants, and cuttings I have collected and lovingly planted throughout the years are like "teens on steroids" and I just cannot. I read somewhere, probably on social media, about these feelings that overwhelm. The "advice" was good, if you cannot do it all just do a little something. Okay.

Today, I chose to clean out a flower bed that runs along a short wall of my house. It was early when I went outside, the Harvest Moon was still shining in the Western sky and the air was cool and smelled like roux – (just joking about the roux). I had fresh energy and dubious determination.

For a while, it was wonderful tending to this little patch of fertile earth early in the morning. I pulled out heaps of wild hydrangea that had spread into infinity and I felt accomplished. This proliferation of Wild Hydrangeas or, as some say, Cashmere Bouquet, is from a few stems my mother brought here about thirty years ago; it is a pass along plant. I remember being so happy to have them (and her) to begin "stocking" my new flowerbeds with plants. My "thirty something" self lovingly planted them in the little butterfly garden I was growing, and all was well. Now, they have put down roots and runners and are never leaving, they are everywhere and my "sixty something" self is overwhelmed. I do not want them to leave because when they bloom in summer and the butterflies come and the air is fragrant from their sweet scent, I stop to think intently of my mother. I never want them to leave, but could they just slow down? Anyway, I pulled all of them out of that bed without regret because I know, for certain, they will be back in the spring and in summer and I will be happy, once again, to see them.

As I pulled and yanked, I was careful not to uproot the daily lilies from Mrs. Viator and vigilant not to accidentally dig up the fat St. Joseph bulbs from Miss Sue. There was a cherished Bleeding-Heart plant that Genie's sisters gifted me soon after she passed and liriope from my mother's house that I did not disturb. In the front yard, there are iron plants I bought years ago from Sr. Ann Carmel; she was having a little plant sale, and these came from the convent's yard...$!.00 a container. I have beautiful Hidden Ginger from Agnes and Louisiana irises from Gus's nursery on HWY. 182, all are growing like children, rapidly, beautifully, and considerably.

Then there is the Creeping Jenny; "Jenny" has crept into the most obscure places and refuses to slow down also, but, in summer, her yellow blossoms are as sweet as her name. She is a pass along plant also (I think from Lonette) with lots of love and beauty attached to her.

I can accurately say "love" covers every inch of my yard, but I must harness it, for unlike the plants, getting older, for me, means slowing down a bit.

Anyway, I recall some parable or story that declares a mouse can eat an elephant one bite at a time. I suppose I can tend to my garden one bed at a time.

While the early morning moon hangs in the Western sky, and the cool air from the North gives me energy, I will pull and dig as

I remember lovingly the people who gave me pass along plants many years ago.

November 20, 2022

It will soon be Thanksgiving Day. I am in a faraway place from my childhood images caused by the vivid lyrics of an old New England poem..." Over the meadow and through the woods to Grandmother's house we go"; I am more into the image of "where did 2022 go"? Weren't we just taking down Christmas trees and getting excited about crawfish and King Cakes? I just cannot understand this sudden speed of time.

That is one reason why I, somewhat, prefer the ordinary days; they tend to move a bit slower, with less urgency. I suppose that must bore many of you, those who love to decorate and celebrate for each holiday. I was once that more spirited person, but not so much anymore, life continues to take us into new chapters, and now, I am here.

I do still like to decorate; just not with store bought things. I love the pile of citrus that will soon be on my kitchen counter after I harvest satsumas, Louisiana Sweets, Ruby Red Grapefruit, and blood oranges from my backyard. The varying shades of yellows and oranges look festive above my Blueberry colored cabinets along with a fat orange pumpkin that escaped the Halloween massacre and sits alone and pompously on a table nearby. And I love the stack of pinecones that will collect near the fireplace and serve as starters for a winter fire. The deep and medium browns against the red bricks of the hearth provide a rustic texture and seasonal aroma along with the green pine needles that will sit along the mantle and contribute to this Christmas "perfume". I especially enjoy the shades of brown, green, and turquoise eggs that sit in a basket in my kitchen, and I appreciate this effort, albeit much less during these shortened days, from my Maran and Americana hens. I enjoy hanging a freshly completed painting on the mustard color wooded knobs of my pantry and living with it a while until I decide if it is finished or not. And I love the way the paper white narcissi bulbs I force will look sitting against the stark coldness that seeps through my kitchen window during Christmas and Hanukah.

I describe all the above with a chuckle and a bit of "tongue in cheek", but I do, essentially, believe it is the little things, the everyday moments that I enjoy the most; the small moments that, for now, measure my life.

Anyway, I also appreciate this written opportunity to wish all of you a Happy Thanksgiving. I hope you have too many blessings to count and not enough room at the Thanksgiving table to seat all the people you love. And I would like to add a wish that we all find a cold morning with hot coffee and a quiet moment to realize our blessings.

On a personal note, it seems I have the most wonderful blessing of all this Thanksgiving, for all my family will be together under one roof for a brief but delightful period of time. I hope to spend much of it holding our newest family member, Santiago... it truly is the little things.

December 4, 2022

Winter is near.

I googled the word "Winter" and learned that it is an Old English word that means "wet and water". I must say, I was a bit disappointed with its lackluster meaning; it seemed so basic. Winter is, indeed, wet; it rains and snows in our hemisphere, but it does much more. Old Man Winter steals the sunlight and robs the earth of its greenness and fertility. Overnight he can turn our spaces into barrenness. Winter can be hard, but winter can also be beautiful.

In South Louisiana, we look forward to those mighty winter fronts that occasionally make it past Interstate 10. We make gumbo and light our fireplaces; we wear our winter gloves and scarves and boots. Perhaps we stay inside and "catch up" with inside chores and projects as we watch the cold winds and misty rain from our windows; it is wonderful...for a while. Somewhere around day three of our "winter", however, I think most will agree, it is time for the sun, it is time to unbundle a bit and get out of the house into the sun.

I seem to have a love hate relationship with winter. I sometimes feel gloomy when it is gloomy, but I welcome the coziness this season gives, the time indoors to start seeds, clean closets, write, paint, and just catch up on domestic chores, for when the sun is out and the weather is mild, I can be no other place than outdoors.

This winter I have a specific plan I would like to share with you, I have a plan to spend time making stocks and soil. I purchase several boxes of organic chicken, beef, and vegetable stock, throughout the year. I use them, as you do, for soups and stews in place of water. They are relatively inexpensive, although they have had a somewhat dramatic price increase, as many other things have. I cleaned out my refrigerator just the other day and found two withered stalks of celery, a small portion of diced bell pepper and onion mix, pieces of what remained of a baked chicken, and three or four carrots in the vegetable bin that, like the celery, had gone limp. I have twelve chickens and I compost, so, that is what I normally do with leftovers that have been forgotten in the refrigerator. But, on that day, I decided to do something different; I would make a stock. I suppose the idea became so appealing because winter is coming and the thought of a homemade stock simmering in my kitchen was pleasing, not to mention, delicious and resourceful.

Along with that idea, I decided to make a batch of soil for my spring and summer garden. I picked a spot in the fenced in part of my garden and began. I have plenty of the brown elements needed because I am a "leave the leaves" gardener and there is an abundance of brown cypress leaves, pine needles, maple, and sycamore leaves in my yard. I also have plenty of the green elements from the kitchen scraps and yard clippings. The third component is water, and I am certain, there will be enough of that this winter. I am missing a pitchfork, however. I am in search of a small one to turn the pile throughout the winter.

Hopefully, when the first signs of spring are here, I have seeds that I have sprouted indoors and a bit of soil to plant each little sapling. I also hope to have a nice supply of stock in my freezer to enhance my soups and stews.

I would like to add to this "productive" little piece that forcing Paper
White Narcissi Bulbs and making Marmalade with our abundant satsuma crops are also two fun and creative "projects" for the colder days ahead.

Bundle up and find the gifts of winter.

January 2023

In these late days of January, days after the killing freeze, I wait for the sun and sneak outside for a bit to see what winter has left. Most of my citrus trees are damaged, but I scratch the surface of the bark and see a vivid green and I have hope, though the leaves that remain are crispy brown and foreboding. There are small oak branches littering the yard, little extensions that could not hold on and there are small green leaves covering my largest fig tree. It is a curious and contrasting sight; this January 2023. I suppose it mirrors much of what will be...curious and contrasting.

There are, once again, many birds. I watch each morning from my kitchen window as they eat amongst the rapid run of the squirrels and the constant pecking of the hens. They blend in just fine, these cardinals and finches and blue jays, enjoying the winter sun and feasting amongst the leaves left from autumn. I have not seen a robin yet. They are, hopefully, still in the woods enjoying their winter diet while awaiting the earthworms to ascend once the ground warms up a bit. I expect them to be fat from the forest. Soon, the groundhog will let us know what is upon us….

I give effort to resting a bit more in winter; it is what nature does, albeit difficult for me sometimes. I treated myself to a favorite (Netflix) movie one afternoon, The Secret Life of Bees. I have seen it before, years ago. I am a self-professed beekeeper, so I was, naturally, drawn into it just from the mention of bees. This time, years later, when I watched it again, the bee factor became just a background to the real substance of the movie. I found much to absorb and learn. I always think a movie, or a book, or a painting is good if it lingers...this one did for me.

The black birds are abundant and nearly deafening. They efficiently fly to the tops of bare trees when I walk near, covering a small portion of the woods, stark and beautiful against the pure blue sky. I suspect this is a good time of year for them, I suspect they enjoy the emptiness the winter provides, I suspect it provides good hunting. Crawfish Holes or Crawfish Chimneys are scattered across the damp field, heralds of Mardi Gras and Lent and all things revered in the South Louisiana winter. It is a cozy look; it is a look of home for all of us. Every year the winter birds come and inhabit our bare trees and the crawfish build their muddy mounds in the wet ground, a protected place to lay their eggs, a place that keeps them safe from predators. Little yellow flowers begin blooming in the same fields, as we wait for the buds on our pecan trees; this is what happens each February in our world. I write about it to honor it, to not let it all happen without a notice, for it is a beautiful annual miracle made just for all of us.

In the middle of this day, I look up and see the moon at its waxing crescent phase, the first phase after the New Moon. It is lovely up there slowly building its glow until it becomes the Full Snow Moon on February 6th. It is all magical and revealing at the same time.

If searching for truth, go outside and watch Nature, for that is where the truth lies.

February 12, 2023

I wish I could remember more about her, like her name. Was she a mother, what kind of house did she live in, how old was she? But I cannot, and it was very long ago and there is no one left to ask. It was the summer of 1974, and I was an art student in Nice, France – the Cote d'Azu. Every weekday morning my friend, Kathy, and I would walk from our room at the Universite de Nice to a second-floor studio with huge windows, wooden easels, and tremendous light. Our journey would take us through the animated and noisy French Market in downtown Nice. There were colorful market umbrellas and plucked chickens hanging upside down, wild rabbits that needed skinning, color wheels of vegetables from the neighboring countryside, Frenchmen speaking quickly and bargaining loudly and there were flowers, buckets, and buckets of fresh cut flowers and everyone bought a bouquet; everyone had fresh flowers on their table each night for dinner. It was intense, this snapshot of life close to the Earth, this snapshot of the sights, sounds, and smells of southern France, a place where the air was sometimes misty, the food was fresh and real, and the people were flourishing and happy under the Mediterranean sun.

The personification of this physical experience could be found in one of our studio models. She too would walk through the market each weekday morning, I would sometimes watch her from one of the oversized windows as she strolled through the dense market, happy and ready to have a wonderful day. Along the way she would gather fresh fruit and baguettes and of course, fresh flowers. She carried it all in an oversized straw basket that was very old, filled with character and the day's supply of food. She wore a summer dress of sorts, one very simple and minimal, for she was a nude model, and she was able to dismiss it without much effort or fumbling. She had sandals on her feet and her hair was long and gray and loosely gathered in a large clip; again, easy to take out and tumble on her shoulders and cast shadows and interesting lines for us to sketch.

The thing I remember most about her was her smile, the radiance she brought to class each morning, as we stood behind our easels, still sleepy from the night before, and there she was with flowers and joie de vivre; content to be exactly where she was. She could not speak much English, but that was okay, her smile spoke of life and passion and happiness.

I remember thinking she seemed to have been "old" to be a model, especially a nude model, but she was so comfortable with who she was; that transformed into her remarkable and memorable beauty.

Strangely, I am probably nearing the age now that she was then and I reflect on who she was; someone, I suspect, who had sorted out all the foolishness in life and was capturing the core each morning, each day with just picked flowers and a freshly baked baguette in her old straw basket, and simplicity in her summer dress and in her life.

March 12, 2023

I am here, still. It is a favorite place, my kitchen. It is a place where I, now, realize life was most 'real' within the boundary of this ordinary room.

My kitchen is the same kitchen I raised my family in; not much has changed. The cabinets are still some shade of blueberry; now, cluttered with remnants of holiday cookie cutters and sippy cups. The 'pantry' has been moved into the keeping room and hides behind mustard-colored doors that are as old as this house. Now and then, I organize the cans of tomato sauce and bags of dried beans, but, mostly, there is little activity in there.

About 30 plus years ago, our kitchen table was replaced with a baker's island of sorts, much smaller by today's standards but big enough by mine. It is where I rolled out breakfast biscuits, decorated homemade birthday cakes, chopped vegetables for soups and supper, paid bills and made my early morning coffee; it has served us well this island crafted by Dalton. Dalton was someone who moved into town and started a woodworking business out of his shop. We read his ad in the newspaper and gave him a try. He has since passed, but his incredible craftsmanship still exists throughout my house, and I am happy to mention his name.

Anyway, not much has physically changed in this hub of home, the kitchen. I know, looking back, this is where much of our lives happened. This is where food was prepared to keep us healthy (at least that was my goal…hoping it would work), and where little hands learned to write and struggle through homework. Late afternoon visits from my dad happened here as did early morning coffee with my mother. Christmas spreads of food lined the crowded counters, and in summer, there were colorful vegetables from the garden ready to be washed and stored. Birthday candles were blown out and Hannukah candles were lit and there were 'make do' vases filled with little bouquets of wildflowers that sat near the sink from a 4-year-old Elizabeth, as did the freshly snapped magnolias from the first days of summer. Many 'little' things happened here...in the kitchen.

Today, the kitchen is less active, but still, it supports our lives, still, it breathes.

I now fill a part of this space with cut flowers and burning candles, baked bread, and a homemade soup in winter; it is a source of comfort and creativity for me. I make lists while sitting on my dad's chair at the island and I still pay my bills here. I am writing this column from the little built-in desk that has been here always. I watch the sun and the full moon set from the window over my sink, where, every year, I see the first robins of spring feasting on the abundant supply of earthworms and the small birds of winter arriving and temporarily covering the ground with their quick little movements as they are passing through. And some days, when I need it most, a cardinal will appear perched on the branches of the Drake Elm.

Real life happens here.

I write this description of my very ordinary 'kitchen', not to be pretentious, but to offer it as a slight pause to, perhaps, appreciate the space that is your "kitchen" ...wherever that may be.

April 2, 2023

Nearly every morning, I sit with coffee in a fat old chair near a window in my studio that looks out into our backyard and into the woods. Some mornings, the moon is there also, perfectly framed by a windowpane looking into my room and reaching into my spirit. Now and then, I miss the instant the sun rises to scatter the new day across the tops of trees, through my windows, and into my conscious and, for me, that is a setback.

These days, in the early morning, there is a bird. He is there right before sunrise calling for his mate with the persistency of a child trying to convince his mother of something inconvincible. I am not sure what sort of bird he is because I cannot find him through the window; he is hidden by the new spring foliage of the trees. But, somehow, we have become "neighbors", he and my dim light through the window are constants. I am curious as to whether he calls for a new mate each morning, if that is indeed what he is doing, or if he is calling for the same. The birds and the bees, such a curious bunch, a bunch we live amongst and many of us know very little about. Anyway, that just happened and now, the coffee is gone, the sun has risen, and the day is here.

Recently, I attended the Plein Air Exhibit and awards ceremony at the Shadows Visitor Center. The art was amazing, but what really captured me was the originality of the artists. Each artist was completely distinguishable. Of course, originality is, in my opinion, one of the main dialogues of good art, but unfortunately, that does not always exist. Here, it was apparent and much appreciated. The skill level was superior, as was the individual interpretations of the quaint and beautiful settings around Acadiana.

I felt happiness knowing there are many 'pieces' from our South Louisiana heritage that still exist as the modern, cookie cutter, big box world slithers in. I often wonder how long 'we' can last, and that wonderment makes me sad. I understand we want more and more conveniences, and more and more stuff is 'needed' to live our modern lives, but these desires of consumption leave little room for the foundations and identities of yesterday.

I cannot blame my opposing attitude on age, for I have always felt this mourning for the depletion of yesterday's defining traditions and physical spaces. I have watched, for years, since 1960, as change occurs; now, it is rapid and exponential. Certainly, good will emerge from these transformations; I just hope we choose to preserve some of our foundation as we tear down much of our surface.

Anyway, the paintings from the show stopped this 'advancement' for just a moment and captured the stillness of time that is Acadiana. Thank you to all the artists that traveled here to share their talents and remind us of the beauty that is Acadiana.

April 16, 2023

Some days I feel a bit 'off'. There is usually nothing terribly 'wrong', but it is, as though, I am out of alignment emotionally.

When I feel that way, I go outside and as I take my first step onto the patio, I feel like Dorothy landing in Oz, kind of. Mother Nature quickly envelopes me with her sights and sounds and her daily rituals. Simple rituals and goings on like a bright green lizard making noise in my unrestrained Peggy Martin that instantly pulls me into this other world of natural magic. At first, I may be startled by the sound, for perhaps it is something unwelcome, but then I see him, busy roaming around looking for breakfast. He has no concern for what is going on in this big wide world, he is busy having his life, basking in the sun, eating bugs, and often, regrowing his tail. I can immediately join him in that perspective, I am in the natural world, and it begins to artfully align my world. I might walk a bit further into the yard to see the monarch caterpillars munching on milkweed knowing that butterflies will be here in summer. I expect they will hover in front of me as I make my way to my garden on early summer mornings to water and again in the later afternoon to gather cucumbers. I will see them as they linger over pink and orange zinnias and bright yellow cosmos eating the nectar fluttering and pollinating, assuring me that later, there will be more blooms in my garden. I might hear the birds chattering about something high in the trees while enjoying the early spring breeze, as their neighbors, the squirrels, jump from tree to tree, hurriedly, as though they had somewhere important to go. They do not care either, they are living their lives and for the most part, joyously. After a walk around the yard, through the woods, perhaps, and a quick check on my garden and chicks, I am usually well-adjusted, once again. It is almost a primal experience, this touch of nature, this feel of something greater than us, this place where life goes on no matter what might be on the 'news'. Nature provides many cures for us but sometimes we forget to pay her a visit. She is my eternal friend.

Dodging the late spring frosts, I have managed to slowly put in my summer garden...a variety of peppers, heirloom tomatoes, cherry tomatoes, cucumbers, an assortment of herbs, Zinnias for Elizabeth's summer cakes, and Milkweed for the monarchs and swallowtails. I am happy with it thus far, but as all gardeners know, it is never complete. Our woods are booming with bunnies and birds by now. I have had to put a bunny proof fence around my vegetable garden and now I deem it a kitchen garden….I love that, it suits my station in life. As a matter of fact, I am 'pulling in' and scaling down as much as I can these days; I want my 'pantry' to be nearby, closer to my backdoor. I am planting fruit trees closer to the house, I have a kitchen garden now instead of multiple rows in the somewhat far away field, my bees and chickens are close and one day, I will, perhaps, be able to move my clothesline near the backdoor. I, too, in this decade of the 60's, must adapt and change just like the green lizard that, by now, may have left the safety of the Peggy Martin and is basking on the rail of the deck and to protect himself, has turned brown.

May 7, 2023

A small, brown table sat in my parent's kitchen for most of my adult life; this is where nearly all my problems were solved. I would sit at one end, my mom would sit on the middle chair and sometimes, my dad would sit on the other end. I would go there for late afternoon coffee nearly every day when my children were growing up. I was able to sit and drink a full cup of coffee without getting up five times; my mom filled in for me.

Throughout the years, this table and this specific chair was where I went to sometimes share happy news and to solve most always many of life's difficulties; they were always there and always listening. I remember a visit after my mother had passed and my dad was terminally ill; I remember my broken heart asking him how I would go on without this place, without this table and my parents around it, for in that moment, I did not know how that could happen.

The years have passed and, obviously, I have made it safely to this point, but the little brown table and two chairs are still here with me.

This is my attempt at a 'Mother's Day' column, while wondering what more can be said about mothers? Beautiful songs have been composed, paintings have been painted, and lovely poems have been written; our mothers are forever in our hearts, two hearts that, once, beat together; our mothers are irreplaceable. My humble words that follow cannot add to anything that has already been said. I can only share a somewhat sweet piece I wrote many years ago when I was raising my own children…

'It began with an eerie dream – pieces of my past all tumbled together ending with me standing in the rain trying to get my daughter where she needed to be.

The symbolism was uncanny – me, spending much of my life holding "umbrellas" over my children, stepping in puddles, and trying to avoid downpours all the while trying to point them towards the light, to a place where they belong, a place where they would be flooded in sunshine. I, and all the moms I know, do this, we "stand out in the rain" and are relentless warriors when our kids are involved. We never stop, no matter how many tears are spilled, and disappointments dealt. Frustrations and discouragements converge and sometimes slow us down, but never stop us, only our last breath can do that.

The moment in the dream was so intense – it was more of a feeling than an actual situation. I am not sure what God was revealing to me – I don't think it was anything specific; I think it was more of a flash of fuel and support – telling me that I needed to keep the umbrella handy and that it was my purpose to protect them , to guide them, no matter how big the storm or how powerful the resistance – I have the "umbrella" and tired as I might be or doubtful as I might feel, I open it each day because I know each day a little rain may fall somewhere. There will be a voice within me, sometimes whispering ever so faintly, but if I am still and am in spirit, I will hear it – this I am sure of.

This is the essence of my dream, and this is the manifestation of its message. Thankfully, the sun is shining as I write this, but my umbrella is there, by the back door."

Mother's Day blessings to all of you, especially the young mothers whose "umbrellas" are nearly always 'open'.

May 28, 2023

I was fine, until I walked into the backyard and saw the little blue pool sitting there...empty. The blue 'shark' was empty also; his days of bubble making were suddenly suspended. It was Thursday morning, very early, early enough to hear the morning birds and tranquil enough to know the neighborhood woodpecker was very busy having breakfast. Most importantly, it was the morning that followed the summer visit from my little Texas family, William, Lorena, Doris, Cami, and Santiago. They most always come in summer. While they are here, I somewhat 'check out' of the real world and try to absorb all that I can that is 'them'. Now, they also bring a little boy, my grandson, Santiago.

He played with toys from the attic, helped me feed the chickens, pointed to the trees (he lives in Midland, so the tall trees are somewhat of an oddity to him), strolled on our quiet street, sang songs on the swing, waved to the friendly lady in the yellow school bus, and swam in a little blue pool. It was four wonderful days of the manifestation of a parent's reward...grandchildren.

Today, the toys will find their way back into the attic, the highchair will go back upstairs, and the little blue pool will become a happy place for my two little ducks to enjoy this summer...my everyday life will move on, but it will be enriched, and the rich memories will linger.

I begin this unofficial "Memorial Day' column with this beautiful, yet tender, personal experience to emphasis how touched we all are by the people we love. We are happy to be with them, for they fit so nicely in our world, and we are sad when they go away.

The sweet little experience I describe is something felt by many grandparents, especially those whose grandchildren and children live far away. It is difficult, but we know there will be another summer, another visit, another time, and another little blue pool...not so for the families who have lost loved ones in service to our country.

This solemn day that society has somewhat reframed as 'the first official day of summer', is an honored national holiday. Trips to the seashore and backyard BBQs are all gloriously American...beautiful days filled with fun, family, and freedom... and while enjoying time off, and anticipating 'all that is summer', I hope we always remember those who made this freedom possible.

I end with a 'reset'...my days of summer are ahead of me, and God willing, I will pick a few more blackberries as I watch the rabbit from the woods scurry quickly from the briar bush when he hears me, I will wake up early to hear the morning birds call for their mates, and water my garden. On sunny days, I will occasionally hang the wash out to dry and I will always have clean water for my baby ducks in Santiago's little blue pool.

July 23, 2023

I am trusting Mother Nature knows what she is doing, but I wish she would 'chill' just a bit. I suppose this heat is doing to us what the extreme cold does to our northern neighbors…forces, those who can, to stay inside for much of the day. I do go outside throughout the day, however. I must. I have discovered that the early morning is my favorite time; it is mild and, if you look and listen, very active and amazing. I know where the sun rises and sometimes, I can find the moon setting, not now, however, for the crescent moon has long ago set when I am outside in the early morning.

The morning is when a 'kettle' of hawks appears …flying over the woods, circling, hunting. They are beautiful and strategic animals, but somehow daunting. I suppose they are looking for field mice; the small mice that run into the woods from the tall grass when I cut the field. My chickens will be starting their day, waiting for the door of the coop to open to begin foraging (and making a mess in my flower beds), and my baby duck is wildly quacking and nervously fidgeting, impatiently waiting for a dip in Santiago's little baby pool. Every morning the small animals that are near me do the same thing, every morning is a new day, and they all seem happy to be here and to begin once again.

The dragonflies and butterflies are feasting in the early morning also, sipping the summer zinnias, skimming the pool, sitting on the clothesline resting and planning their next attack. The birds are especially noisy in the early morning, talking to one another, making plans and flirting. And the squirrels are jumping from limb to limb already making mayhem in the pecan trees, already eating the green pecans I will never be able to crack. It is a very busy place this early morning scene.

If I attempt to go outside in the middle of the day, when temperatures reach the mid to upper nineties, I hear the deafening sound of the cicadas. I image they are happy in this heat, but I do not know that for sure. My chickens are, by the afternoon, just basking in a dirt bath they have made for themselves or hiding out in the shade, bellies somewhat full of the morning bug fests. My little duck is a new feature in my tiny menagerie, so I am not certain of his routine yet. I know he quacks incessantly and has beautiful iridescent feathers and eats a lot more than my chickens; he is cute and greedy. I am not out for long in the middle of the day; it is difficult to be that hot.

The evening slowly spins in, and it is nice again. The new moon happened this past Monday. As you read this the moon will be five days old and a waxing crescent...growing until it is full again on August 1, the Full Sturgeon Moon. It is one of my favorite things in life, no kidding, watching the moon. It seems stoic and calm sitting there in the heavens observing. It has 'seen' everything, it has watched the Earth grow and change and it has witnessed all that mankind has endured, caused, and done. Don't hate me for this or think I am foolish, but I somehow wish we had never landed there...its mystery disappeared with that first human step. I suppose it was a good thing that all those beautiful songs were written about the celestial orb before man walked on it, for now, the enigma and romance are somewhat gone.

And then evening falls, the world quietens, and the sun submits. People come out of their houses to water plants, ride bicycles, and Mother Earth becomes kind once again. A different medley of birds appears and can be heard in the tops of the trees. My bees are returning from their long journey, returning with pollen baskets on their tiny legs to bring to the hive. My chickens are finding their way back to the coops and roosting for the night; their day is done.

I watch the sun go down, sometimes hear the mosquito truck, lock up my hens and duck, and anxiously await the new day so we can, hopefully, do it all over again.

I close with a wish that you all manage to find a bit of beauty in these Dog Days of summer.

It's hot.

September 3, 2023

I was there for the Blue Moon. I had completed a day filled with the preciousness of Santiago. It was a day at the Children's Museum and swinging in the park and eating noodles for lunch and blowing bubbles in the backyard; it was a day that was the best day. That night, the Full Moon rose in a clear West Texas sky and, in the most breathtaking way, closed the door on this special memory.

It was as if an old friend had followed me across Texas to Midland, making sure this near perfect day was capped off with 'the light of the silvery moon'.

I am home again, and it is September, the transitional month. It offers an informal farewell to summer on Labor Day and slowly tiptoes into autumn, sometimes tempting us with a cool morning and a gumbo kind of evening.

All my little summer 'friends' have grown so big by now. The languid lizards of summer are still there, basking and eating, but they are now full grown and brave. I see them out in the open more often than hiding in bushes and behind flowerpots as they did in spring when they were little. They have managed to survive and with survival, they have gained confidence and mindfulness. The dragonflies of summer are huge. Their wingspan has grown significantly, and I feel confident they have eaten hundreds of mosquitos, perhaps thousands, and for that, I am so grateful. The June bugs are long gone, and the tiny hummingbirds are here for a little bit of time. I have several saucers and containers throughout my yard for the honeybees, for their water sources have been depleted. They gather each morning and hang out throughout the day; it is an amazing sight, the systematic flight patterns, and their attachment to the water. I feel happy I can, somewhat, accommodate these little creatures that work so hard and are essential to our existence. The trees are changing also. They are slowly dropping leaves and changing colors; the bloom of summer is over.

Nature is my source of strength and encouragement. Sometimes I get overwhelmed by the 'news' and the twisted way I see the world. When I do, I step outside, and all is suddenly right side up again. I walk into nature's borough, into a place where everything is real, and all is as it should be. The virtual world of deceit quickly fades away and I am reminded of the important things in my life.

As wonderful as Mother Nature is, she has been known to 'turn on us' in September. This is the month where the likelihood of a hurricane is present; hopefully we will escape the wrath of the warm Gulf.

I end with a plea from the honeybees to set a saucer or two of fresh water outside for them and a heartfelt wish for all our farmers to have a wonderful beginning and ending to their harvest; a perfect season should happen 'once in a Blue Moon'.

September 2023

They scattered and shared four o'clock seeds and exchanged recipes, recipes that were written on slips of paper and the blank backs of old envelopes. My mother's generation has silently slipped away, but the lessons we learned from the lives they lived will, hopefully find its way into this modern world of virtuality and illusion.

I am prompted to write about this time from long ago for two reasons, I was looking for a recipe for chicken salad in an old Betty Crocker cookbook and because one of my mother's dear neighbors and friends recently passed, Miss Zella. It caused a stir, it made we face the fact that 'they' are gone, their way of doing things, their sometimes frugality and resourcefulness that existed within their homes, their domestic poise, their generation, gone. So much is lost, so much humanity has been replaced. Some of you will think that is a good thing, modern conveniences taking the place of all that these women, our mothers, spent their days doing; I question it all, however. These women cloaked us in the fabric of home. They wore house dresses with pockets and used Maybelline mascara in a small red box with a tiny brush, they dusted furniture with Old English and old T-shirt fabric, they wrote checks and read Little Golden Books to us. And they visited, real visits not quick texts and FB post. They made friends with neighbors and had coffee at one another's houses while we played outside and drank Kool aide.

I have those fragile and warm memories of my mother and even a few tangible things.

Her 4 o'clocks are still growing in my yard and there are her handwritten recipes tucked in cookbooks in my kitchen. And when I pass by the scarlet flower and its fragrance scatters in the air, I only think of her. And when I dig around in a recipe box and find My mother's cursive script on a torn sheet of notebook paper. There she is once again, she is with me for a moment, explaining the recipe, being my mom.

On a kitchen shelf is a very old recipe 'book', something with broken spirals, something I have had since early marriage, something that holds tight so many memories from people I once knew...dear dear people. I have Miss Dot's bread and butter pickles 2 $\frac{1}{2}$ pints, Miss Helens pickled okra, Genie's Mexican cornbread, my grandmother's Chow chow, my aunt's aunt La La cake, my mom's gingersnaps, and Susan crawfish fettuccini. It was like reuniting with these people as I went through the little broken and tattered book.

Anyway, this experience, this personal touch, I fear is soon to be gone, if not already. We now have Google. No more handwritten recipes from people we spent the times of our lives with women who turned out beautiful food each day and were always passing along tips, recipes, and 4 o'clock seeds.

October 1, 2023

It is such a safe little corner, this place I go to each morning. I can sometimes see the weary moon through the window or hear the last calls of the owl as I sit in my overstuffed chair with coffee and watch as the day breaks, unsealing the unknown pieces of my life.

It is a curious time, this beginning of, yet another day. On this particular morning, I think of my dad; it would be his 93rd birthday. I smile as I remember how he would joke that his birthday was celebrated throughout the town with a fair and festival and how, as a child, I must have believed him. Mostly, I remember that he could 'fix' things, my bike, later, my car, and many times, my life. Happy birthday, dad...wish you were here.

October, however, is here. It is one of my favorite months of the year. The Full Harvest Moon showed us its majesty, gumbo weather is on the way, and Golden Rods are soon to cascade over the little fence Matt and Drew built years ago around Elizabeth's butterfly garden (thanks Miss Leah for the inspiration). The Golden Rods will flower soon and provide a spicy nectar for my bees, happiness swarms and brims.

I will take a picture of this small and wonderful spot in my yard and my thoughts will leave the day for a while and return to my parent's house in autumn with my little boys in corduroy pants and little navy caps that snapped. Not sure why, but that will happen. Somehow, the hints of autumn cause nostalgia.

With the thermometer reading 89, it may seem impossible, but if you listen carefully to the distant whispers of the wind, you will know that the season is changing; summer is leaving, and autumn is slowly and muskily rolling in. The squirrels, by now, have eaten my pecans, the leaves on the Crepe Myrtles are turning orange and brown and beginning to fall, and if you are outside early, you can feel this elusive change.

I hope this season of pumpkin spice and colorful foliage stays a while for it is a busy time in the garden and in the home, time to put garlic cloves in the ground, scatter lettuce seeds, and put a fat orange pumpkin at our doors as we whisk away the summer.

Allow me to close with an autumn memory, something so sweet and simple, something that technology has, unfortunately, taken…

When my children were little, my dad would call me (on the land line), to let me know The

Great Pumpkin Charlie Brown would be on TV, making sure they did not miss this holiday tradition….it is the little things I miss the most.

November 26, 2023

It is early Thanksgiving morning and as the sun rises, the holiday season begins. Grace will be said at Thanksgiving tables and boxes of decorations will come down from attics, here we go…

I almost always begin the holiday season with Narcissus bulbs. On a day near Thanksgiving, I begin 'forcing' ten to twelve bulbs into a container filled with rocks and water. The planted bulbs will sit under my kitchen window until late January; they are my winter 'guests'. I watch them grow each day thereafter as I work in the kitchen. They are beautiful up against the amber landscape just outside of the window. As the days pass and Christmas comes near, these dainty paperwhites will bloom. Their blooms carry on into the new year. Once their leaves begin to sprawl and flop, it is time to move them into a more beneficial environment, the yard.

The planting part of this humble holiday ritual begins with choosing an arbitrary spot. This usually happens on a January day that is somewhat mild. I turn over soil and plant about three or four of the bulbs, crudely cover, and repeat until all are planted. I have thirty-plus little bouquets of Narcissus flowers that pop up each year in late winter or very early Spring. They faintly scent the thin winter air and remind me of Christmases of long ago…a small tradition I somewhat created for myself that connects me to the winter landscape, counts the years I have been here, and pulls in memories of people I love, especially my mother, for those were her favorite flowers.

So begins my winter kitchen. Later, there will be Echinacea pods and Zinnia seeds on my windowsill, drying in the gentle afternoon sun, and a sparse amount of the remaining basil from my small garden hanging alongside the thriving oregano, ready to enrich something Italian like a spaghetti sauce or minestrone.

Usually, my counters are filled with an array of citrus, enough to last through February but, the late killing freeze last March was brutal, and my trees did not do well. I do have my Evangeline sweet potatoes, thanks to Jimmy and Flo Broussard who made, yet another trek to St. Landry parish to purchase those sweet spuds directly from the farmer. Those ample boxes of sweet potatoes will sit near the back door until early December, curing, waiting for the release of their sweetness, and then into the oven, baking and filling my kitchen with the fragrance of Ville Platte memories of my mammae's kitchen.

Perhaps a bit of musty fall honey will be harvested before the end of the year. Or we may just leave an extra bounty for my bees.

Eventually, there will be a vintage Santa that Erik found in a second-hand store and gifted me one Christmas. The timeworn Kris Kringle will once again stand near the fireplace in the keeping room and keep me company on the days before Christmas and I will miss his jolly presence when Christmas is gone. A cedar tree, hopefully from the woods, will be sparsely but caringly decorated and, in early December, a menorah will be lit.

My unassuming winter kitchen will be filled with the simple delights of the season and an abundance of gratefulness for the life I have been blessed with.

Soon, Nature will display her beautiful bareness. We will see through the trees, past the naked branches and the reveal of the imperfect trunk, the trunk that has literally 'weathered the storm' and while scarred and blemished, stands tall. It continues to do its job giving us shade in summer, fallen leaves in autumn, and in winter, we learn its secrets, but in spring, we see tiny green buds and, once again, it gives us hope.

As this holiday season 'takes off', I hope for joyous moments with family and friends, a simple winter kitchen filled with the scents and sights of home, and peace on earth…

December 10, 2023

I heard an owl hooting a bit after midnight; I suppose it was he who woke me up. He was in the maple tree in the backyard, near the bedroom window. It is a great spot for an owl; my chickens live near there and offer the owl deceptive hope for a generous midnight feast and an old compost bed rich with earthworms and insect carcasses still exists near there. My chickens are locked safely in their nighttime cages; sorry Mr. Owl, but they will not be hunted by you. But the small field mice, the ones that I hear in the evening roaming through the cavities of the firewood rack and squeaking, precious, tiny squeaks that make people say 'eek', I fear, are not safe. They will be successfully sought.

I could not fall back asleep after I heard the hooting owl. It was impossible, the freeway in my head started…scenes from the day before collected, concerns of the day ahead encircled, episodes and situations from childhood, mine, and my children, sat there waiting for stringent evaluation, virtual packing for a trip took place, and then there was the owl. To fall back into sleep, my annoying nocturnal thoughts landed there, with the hooting owl. I thought of him in wonder… how did he become associated with wisdom and where was he throughout the day? And the forlorn hooting, what was that about? It was an expected sound, a pureness of the natural world…a hooting owl, but why? Anyway, like the owl, sleep did not come…

Within my somewhat desolate nocturnal thoughts, I thought of a quick snapshot from long, long ago, from 1962. It was of a tree and a place. I was a child, and much was different then. The natural world was a fundamental part of my life. There were trees everywhere with Spanish moss hanging from their ancient and regal boughs and only scatterings of farmhouses could be seen in the countryside and the stores were all on Main Street and filled with shoppers on Saturdays; it was a quaint and beautiful town with unique customs and friendly people, it was the Queen City on the Teche. I lived in a place surrounded by woodland, a new subdivision called Little Woods. It seemed far away from everything; it was near Bayou Teche and just a few families lived there.

My restless thoughts continued and brought me to a place across a very old bridge. There was a small structure near the soon-to-be replaced bridge; I suppose a bridge-keeper lived there and there was a general store at the end of the road. The store was old and wooden and off the ground. It was framed by massive Live Oak trees and seemingly in the middle of nowhere. My mother would take me there sometimes for corn suckers...a sucker crudely shaped like a corn cob and in it, sometimes, if you were lucky, was a coin, a penny, or a nickel. I suppose she would buy a bit of groceries there also; I just remember the grape-flavored corn sucker.

My memory is so slight and foggy and my mother, my historian, is not here to help me with the recollection, but I do remember the feeling of that very old store. It was dark and silent inside and there was a long wooden counter where the corn suckers were. Then, one day not long after, the old store was gone.

Sadly, I have just learned the ancient Live Oak tree that stood next to it, is, now, gone also. It was there for over a hundred years, a link to our past and an icon of our culture. It bravely weathered hurricanes and avoided lightning strikes and sat there near the Teche quietly and majestically offering a home for owls and squirrels and beauty for the passersby. Soon, there will be no memory of the old store or the majestic tree.

Soon, cement and consumerism will be all we see and all we know.

December 24, 2023

I am sitting down to write, early, during these pre-dawn moments of the Winter Solstice, December 2023. I am waiting for the sunrise while still encapsulated in the aura of night. Christmas will soon be here.

Each Christmas brings new circumstances, new events, and occurrences, both in our world and within our families. This Christmas our world is brazenly flashed across the screens of our lives and is volatile and tense. I would never attempt to comment on any of that, for I find it hard to find truth, much that we see is an illusion. Anyway, while trying to create a column, I looked through my document folders and I found a Sunday column from 2011. It was Christmas day, and I wrote about the place I was in. Twelve Christmases later, almost all have changed...life moves on with rapidity and people come and go places change, and beginnings and endings are there waiting in the wings. I resubmit this time and place to illustrate, to emphasize...to 'enjoy the now'.

December 25, 2011

In my kitchen, there are a few precocious camellias floating in a clear bowl of water, brought in from the barren winter yard. There are fresh-picked oranges and the last of the Satsumas scattered about, the narcissi bulbs I began forcing the day after Thanksgiving are struggling to bloom but are fat and about to open nonetheless, the Menorah has been lit for 5 nights, the Fraser fir is looking a bit weary but still sending the fragrance of Christmas throughout the house, the Advent calendar is donned and completed and so, I think, it must be Christmas Day. I have collected many Christmas memories for Christmas 2011 and hopefully, they will carry me through with a spirit of joy and hope until next year.

My memories do not center around the mall or online shopping sites, those places wreck it for me, instead, they are about people I have met and places I have been.

One recent evening, Skip and I found our way to a wonderful place in the country near the village of Loreauville, Gerald Judice's woodworking shop. It was a visit that was unplanned, just a random call on a December evening. We spent a long while there for there was so much to see and so many wonderful things to hear and learn, like what kind of pecan trees to plant, tips on growing strawberries, how to protect citrus from freezing temperatures, and how the bluebird population has curiously increased in Loreauville. He showed us beautiful bowls his daughter, Emily, had, just that afternoon, made and crosses Lauren created from pieces of cypress and mahogany. I even came home with scraps of sunken cypress and beautiful mahogany to use for the "peace" crosses I am currently painting – it was like visiting Santa's workshop for me – so many treasures were there, so much creativity and craftsmanship to absorb. We also left with blood oranges and bunches of broccoli to eat and juice and pecans for nibbling and baking. What a magical interruption from the hyper-consumerism that is the Holidays.

Then, there was the late December afternoon and a cup of hot tea and wistful conversation in my kitchen with my friend Tere – a conversation rooted in history and words spoken in a way that takes time, time that only old friends can know.

I spent time with family, something I do not ever take for granted; they are here, and all is well with my world. My brother, sister and I keep alive the memories of our parents while continuing to make memories of our own, each somehow directed by their inspiration, bringing a piece of our past to this Christmas present.

I have experienced the gambit of emotion this holiday season from missing my parents and those days of childhood when the whole world was sprinkled with magic dust and later, those days as a young mother when I got to do it all again - kissing tiny faces late on Christmas Eve night knowing how filled up with anticipation and wonderment they were. All those days and these days are bundled together and have taken me here; here at this very moment writing this very story…everything matters.

Okay that's it, the Christmas bells are ringing for now it's Christmas Day - nothing else can be done; it's here. Relax. The goose is in the oven, the living room is covered with wrapping paper and memories, and the family is on their way, "may your hearts be merry and bright…

January 2024

Funny how we sometimes dream of summer in winter and winter in summer… I think I am doing that now on this gray day in late January. I managed to walk around in the swampy yard yesterday, capturing a few moments of the sun's stingy rays, hurdling through shallow puddles of rainwater, too much moisture for the mighty Earth to absorb. My little duck was having a wonderful time in the said puddles, flapping her wings, and splashing in these welcoming pools of water. I suppose there is always something positive to find in our days; my little duck made me smile. My chickens were not so happy, however. Finding bugs to snack on is not an easy job these days…life gives and takes.

The bit of sunlight began to fade, and I went back inside, for it was still a little cold from the recent temperature drop, at least I thought so. Inside was still and winter. Nothing was on the stove, the laundry room was quiet by now, and the TV was off. I could hear only the familiar chimes from the mantle clock and the seconds ticking on the small red clock near my desk. I had, by now, forgotten the brief happiness my little duck had brought me and became more introspective. Oddly, I began thinking of my mother in summer. I thought of her in a way that grabbed my heart, an unexpected throwback, a resurfacing of grief that hit me suddenly, a moment that made losing her raw again, nearly twenty-seven years later.

I remembered the seemingly endless summer days when I was a young mother. I spent much time with her; she was there to help me with my small children and listen to my life. Summer was hot, she wore sleeveless button-down shirts and pulled her hair up. And she made Kool-Aid for my little boys, drip coffee for me, and pinned my little girl's busy bangs up in a pin curl, pulling a random bobby pin from her hair to do that. She sat on her front porch swing with Elizabeth while she listened carefully to all I had to say.

I think of those gentle moments that are visiting me on this winter day and I know we all share this kind of loss. I 'go with it", I let myself become sad and I saturate my mind and memory with her and try hard to remember more. A jumbled scattering of her words floods my thoughts and I recall the seemingly little 'nothings' she spoke and know now, those 'nothings' were messages for me, things to remember for later when she would not be here...deeper and deeper I go.

After a while, it becomes enough melancholia, and I am here again on this January day, in my life, feeling a bit more like my little duck...happy to have taken that somewhat sad but reflective journey and grateful for the wonderful memories, always wishing there were more.

I suppose our lives become a collection of moments, seemingly small moments that we stitch together, as they become our tapestry that later becomes our memories. These memories surface unexpectedly, especially in winter when the world is quiet, and my mother in summer becomes a small dream I have in winter...

February 24, 2024

My dad had just passed away when I began this Second Front column in 2006. It was a difficult time, the time when you move to the top of the family totem pole….Skip and I were suddenly the oldest in our extended family. There was no one who knew more about our family history and the intricate little morsels of our lives. My mom, and now my dad were no longer here.

Writing has always been a source of harmony for me and when my dad died, it became (nearly) vital. I was able to put thoughts on paper, as I had done for most of my adult life, but now I could share them, thanks to Will Chapman at the Daily Iberian. He gave me an opportunity to share a small amount of newsprint with Morris Raphael; I am forever grateful for the chance he gave me and the guidance he provided.

Anyway, here it is the start of 2024, eighteen years later. My five children are all adults now and Skip and I have been blessed with a precious grandchild, Santiago. I live in the same house, but my garden has moved closer to my backdoor and is much smaller, I have retired from teaching, and I still miss my parents each day. While I have enjoyed my small and humble contribution to the Daily Iberian, it is time to write the last Berry Tale. This will be my final Sunday column.

It is still winter as I write this, but signs of spring are showing up in the fields and in my garden. I have yet to see a robin come from the woods or a tiny baby lizard, but my fig trees are budding, and sunset has found its way into my keeping room later in the day, scattering dappled sunlight and bringing joy and promise of yet another spring. My windowsills are crowded with tiny saplings in little pots of soil…heirloom tomatoes, an array of peppers, herbs, and, just for fun, sweet peas (Sister Ann Carmel's sweet peas were the centerpiece of my first column) …I love the circles life makes.

The Full Snow Moon will rise on the 24th and spring will arrive on the 19th of March.

As anxious as we all are for spring, I hope you enjoy these last days of winter, for each season is beautiful.

p.s. I feel presumptuous writing the following, but I shall anyway…I have by luck and chance been able to have a small paperback published. The title is Bayou Shadows, and it is listed as a fictional memoir. It is expected to be out within the year. I began the process in August of 2022…it has been a very long, but worthwhile, journey, a bucket list 'check off' for sure.

Also, I plan to continue my random musings and posting on my webpage, pamshenskyart.com, if you are ever lonesome for newsflashes about what might be going on in my backyard (lol).

The End

Thank you to all who have followed me throughout these years. My gratitude is immeasurable.

Made in the USA
Columbia, SC
28 July 2024